Portraying Finland

FACTS AND INSIGHTS

Portraying Finland

FACTS AND INSIGHTS

OTAVA PUBLISHING COMPANY LTD

HELSINKI

VIRTUAL.
FINLAND.FI
· YOUR WINDOW ON FINLAND ·

Second, revised edition

Editorial Board:
Laura Kolbe (Editor-in-Chief)
Juha Parikka
Liisa Suvikumpu (Picture Editor)
Eva Reenpää
Marita Jaakkola

Graphic design and layout: Timo Numminen
English translation: Malcolm Hicks and William Moore

Printed by:
Otava Book Printing Ltd
Keuruu 2008

ISBN 978-951-1-22420-4

European integration, free market economics and globalization have entered the history of many countries over the past ten years and national political programmes and self-images have altered, sometimes radically, since the end of the Cold War. Finland has perhaps not had to go through a sharp reorientation, but nonetheless people here are asking, "Who are we? Where have we come from? How are we going to manage in this new situation?"

Geography and history have always exercised a great influence on how Finland has been perceived. Geography has been invoked to describe features such as the natural environment, the climate, landscapes, regions and peoples, while history has recounted the beginnings of human settlement, social development and nationhood. As times have changed, the emphases in this narrative have altered. Especially at moments of political upheaval it has been felt to be important to describe how the country has gained its constitutional status and distinctive character.

Finland is...
...the cycle of the
seasons, originality
in architecture,
Helsinki Cathedral,
yachts, farmhouses,
snowdrifts, blue and
white colours.

Portraying Finland is the latest in a long line of books published for the purpose of explaining Finland to others as a country, nation, culture, and society. Its face has traditionally been the face of nature, but no longer. It is now an urban, post-industrial society, technically and technologically among the most advanced in the world. At the same time "green" values and a longing to preserve contacts with nature have attained a higher priority than ever. Even though Finland is still situated at a cultural cross-roads between north and south, east and west, these new times call for a new appraisal of its essential nature.

The writing and editing of this book have been the outcome of fruitful cooperation involving a large number of people. The content was planned by a trio comprising **Juha Parikka,** Director of Publishing of the Finnish Ministry for Foreign Affairs, **Eva Reenpää**, Publishing Manager of the Otava Publishing Company, and the undersigned. The writers represent the peak of expertise in their own fields, many of them having done a great deal of work as teachers or social and political commentators to explain their country's history and alignment.

Dr. Jukka Tarkka is a well-known political analyst, freelance writer and journalist, **Dr. Allan Tiitta** is docent in human geography at the University of Helsinki, **Jyrki Vesikansa Lic.Phil.,** is a journalist and writer on current affairs, **Prof. Markku Wilenius** is director of the Finland Futures Research Centre at the Turku School of Economics and Business Administration and **Dr. Henrik Meinander** and the undersigned are professors of history at the University of Helsinki. The picture editor was **Liisa Suvikumpu M.A.,** likewise of the University of Helsinki. To all these people I extend my grateful thanks for their skilful work.

Laura Kolbe
Editor-in-Chief

Januarius. Tamikwla on xxxi.

pâiue / O ô pite xvj hetke. pâiue pite viij
hetke Auringo nâuse liki viij ia laskehen
liki iiij Cuulla ombi xxx pâiue.

#							
1	xix	Calē	A	Ci	Wden wodē pâiue	*	A
2	viij	iiij	b	si			b
3		iij	c	o		*	c
4	xvi	ij	d	Ja			d
5	v	nonas	e	nus		*	e
6		viij	f	ep	Colmē pyhen Kuni		f
7	xiij	vij	g	ca	Knwtin kunnigā	*	g
8		vj	A	si			h
9	ij	v	b	bi			i
10	x	iiij	c	ven			k
11	xviij	iij	d	di	Solin aquario		l
12		ij	e	cat			m
13	vij	Idus	f	oc			n
14		xix	g	fe	felix pappi		o
15	xv	xviij	A	li	Maurus abboti		p
16	iiij	xvij	b	mar	Marcell9 martir		q
17		xvj	c	an	Anthonius abboti		z
18	xij	xv	d	pris	Prisca Neitzyt		r
19		xiiij	e	fab	Fabianus ia Sebass		s
20	i	xiij	f	hen	Heyneriki Bispa		s

1

History

Finland was under Swedish rule for 600 years. It was an autonomous Grand Duchy in the Russian Empire from 1809 to 1917, became independent from 1917, and has been associated with the western cultural sphere since the 12th century. It has had a special relationship with Russia from the 18th century and a history influenced by the fluctuating balance of power in Europe and the Baltic region.

As well as having been a leading figure of the Reformation, Mikael Agricola is regarded as the father of written Finnish. One of his main works was the *Rukouskirja* (Prayer Book) of 1544. Its 877 pages were widely used by the clergy. Not content with providing saints' days and tables for calculating the dates of other religious festivals in the calendar section, he also included basic information on the Ptolemaic view of the world, astrology, the chemical elements, and the treatment of diseases.

A PART OF THE KINGDOM OF SWEDEN

In spite of its easterly location, in cultural terms Finland developed as a part of western Europe. Since the Roman Empire never expanded to include the northernmost reaches of Europe, Christianity in the shape of the Roman Catholic Church took root in Finland and in Scandinavia only in the 9th and 10th centuries.

In the Finnish case, the landfall of Christianity coincided with the country's becoming increasingly bound to the kingdom of Sweden. The connection was strengthened in stages, and by the beginning of the 16th century the southwestern reaches of modern Finland had become a constituent part of Sweden. This was to have far-reaching consequences for the later development of the country as a whole. The social framework, values, and everyday practices of Western civilisation took root in the country. At the same time, the southern and western coastal areas were settled by a Swedish-speaking minority that exists in Finland to this day.

In 1527, noticing that his treasury coffers were empty, King Gustav Vasa of Sweden followed the example of the north German princes. The property of the Roman Catholic Church was seized, citing Martin Luther's theses, which argued among other things that the church was a commonwealth of believers, and that as such its wealth and property should belong to the people.

The King's rift with Rome grew permanent over the decades that followed, and as a consequence Finland – the eastern part of the Swedish realm – became the northeastern fringe of Protestant Europe. The Reformation also brought with it significant steps towards the emergence of Finnish as a written language. In 1548 Mikael Agricola, one of the leading proponents of the Protestant Reformation in Sweden-Finland, released his Finnish translation of the New Testament. The synthesis of dialects, mainly from western Finland, paved the way for the modern Finnish language.

By the end of the 16th century, roughly 300,000 people were living in Finland. Half of them were settled along the coastline in the southwestern corner of the country and lived by farming and fishing. The other half lived mainly from slash-and-burn agriculture,

Legend has it that the English-born Bishop Henry who came to christianise Finland was killed by a local peasant at Köyliö some time in the 1150s. He is now recognised as a national saint and there are statues and paintings of him in many churches and museums.

reindeer herding, and from hunting in the much more extensive forested areas found further inland. The seven major centres of population included Turku, the seat of the Bishop of Turku, Viipuri (Vyborg), the gateway to eastern Finland, and Helsinki, which had been founded by Gustav Vasa in 1550, as a rival to Tallinn. Helsinki was initially a dismal failure and of little real significance – its importance grew only in the latter part of the 18th century with the building of the massive offshore fortress of Viapori (known since 1918 as Suomenlinna).

Finland's location as the eastern outpost of Swedish power had its own price. From the 15th century, Russia developed into a unified state that was to wage repeated wars with its western neighbours over the centuries that followed. Sweden was one such adversary, having first grown during the 16th century into the dominant power in the Baltic Sea region and then in the 17th

When the principality of Muscovy began its expansion in the late 15th century, a new castle named Olavinlinna, after the Norwegian Saint Olaf, was built to protect the eastern border of Finland. Having become something of a national symbol in its time, it is now the venue for the annual Savonlinna Opera Festival.

century into an important geopolitical player on the larger European stage.

The Great Northern War of 1700–1721 saw Sweden lose its Baltic hegemony in favour of an emergent Russia. This had a decisive influence on Finland, for in 1703 – after taking land back from Sweden – the Russian Tsar Peter the Great founded St. Petersburg at the eastern end of the Gulf of Finland. Peter established the city on the River Neva as the new capital, and St. Petersburg rapidly grew into a northern European metropolis.

And as St. Petersburg gained in stature, so Finland's geopolitical position became increasingly important for both Sweden and Russia. The huge fortress of Viapori, whose name in Swedish – *Sveaborg* – means "Sweden's Fortress", was built just off the coast facing Helsinki with help from the French, specifically to counter Russian expansionism and the threat of the large Russian naval base at Kronstadt, just outside St. Petersburg.

However, when the countries found themselves at odds once again in 1808–1809, as part of the diplomatic chain reaction of the Napoleonic Wars, this great "Gibraltar of the North" proved to be of little worth. The Russians surrounded and bombarded the fortress, forced an early surrender, and in the Treaty of Fredrikshamn (Finnish *Hamina*) in September 1809 all of Finland was annexed as part of the burgeoning Russian Empire.

Turku was an important town in the Kingdom of Sweden, with its own cathedral, bishop's see, and chapter house. In Finland today it is regarded as a symbol of historical continuity and European urban culture. The originally Roman Catholic cathedral, dedicated to the Virgin Mary and St. Henry, has become truly a national monument.

A GRAND DUCHY OF THE RUSSIAN EMPIRE

At the beginning of the 19th century, Russia was not a unified state in administrative terms, but rather more a patchwork of many states under the formal control of the imperial rulers. Hence Finland, which was given the status of an Autonomous Grand Duchy, was allowed to maintain its Lutheran religion and its Swedish

FROM THE STONE AGE ONWARDS

There is no shortage of starting-points for the history of Finland. If one settles on the history of the region's population as a base line, things began around 9,000 BC. During the last Ice Age, the whole of northern Europe was covered by a thick layer of ice that was two to three kilometres deep across the area that is modern-day Finland. When this ice-sheet began to melt and retreat, and as the Finnish mainland slowly rose above sea level, hunters in search of game wandered into the region from the southeast and also from the north. We do not know what language or languages they spoke. Many scholars theorise that the migrants from the southeast would already have spoken a variant of Proto-Uralic, the linguistic ancestor of modern Finnish. Proto-Uralic, which subsequently split into several sub-families of languages, was the common tongue across the northern regions of European Russia. Whatever the truth of this theory, gradually the various dialects of this "ur-Finno-Ugric" tongue developed into the permanent language of those living in Finland, even though new inhabitants had constantly been flowing into the area from different points of the compass.

The Stone Age inhabitants left rock paintings of animals and human figures. They drew particular inspiration from the elk, as have modern Finnish jewellery designers.

15

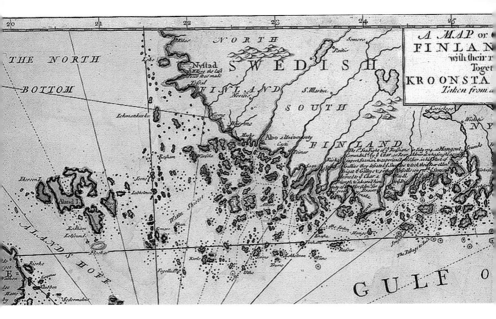

The Gulf of Finland increased in strategic importance in the eighteenth century, when the city of St. Petersburg was built at its eastern end. This meant that power centres of east and west at that time were linked along the axis St. Petersburg – Turku – Stockholm.

administrative culture, and in addition was even given its own government – the Senate – and a Minister-Secretary of State who presented Finnish affairs directly to the Tsar in St. Petersburg. To crown things off, Tsar Alexander I attached to the Grand Duchy the Karelian Isthmus, which had been taken from Sweden in the Great Northern War a hundred years earlier.

In order to strengthen the union and safeguard against influence from Sweden, in 1812 Alexander further decided to move the capital of his Grand Duchy from Turku to Helsinki, and he simultaneously ordered the comprehensive rebuilding of the city.

Senate Square and the buildings bordering its four sides formed the nucleus of a new and handsome neoclassical city centre that was familiar from the likes of Berlin or St. Petersburg but quite unprecedented in Finland. Over the decades that followed, a vibrant administrative city grew up, with a regular grid pattern. Helsinki's weight and significance was further increased in 1827, by the relocation there of the Royal Academy of Turku (founded in 1640), Finland's only university at the time. Its new name, The Imperial Alexander University, was a bold statement of its new status.

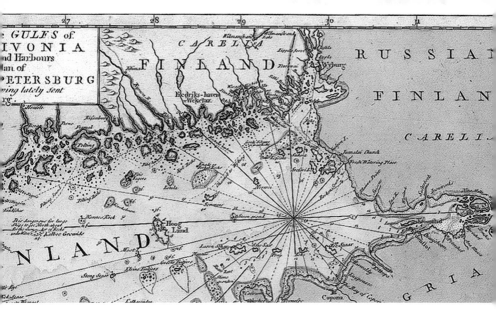

The Russian rulers saw Finland primarily as a northwestern outpost of their domain, and in the early decades of the 19th century many in Finland also imagined that the country would gradually be absorbed into the ever-expanding Russian Empire. This was not to be: the Swedish social framework, the separate administrative culture that supported this, and the continued trade connections with the former motherland ensured that Finland's distinctive features remained very much alive. When nationalist ideals began

Finland's first university was founded in Turku in 1640. Following the Great Fire of Turku it was relocated in 1828 to Helsinki, which by that time had become the capital.

17

Colourful costumes indicate the areas from which their wearers come. Albert Edelfelt's painting *Women Outside the Church at Ruokolahti* (1887) depicts a group of women in Karelian regional dress conversing by the church wall.

to take root in the country from the 1840s, this "separate path" was also given a very solid ideological foundation. The pioneering figures of Finnish nationalism were above all Elias Lönnrot, the folklorist and compiler of the national epic *Kalevala* (1835), the poet J. L. Runeberg, and the philosopher and senator J.V. Snellman, who demanded that Finnish replace Swedish as the country's first language, both in administrative matters and in culture.

By the end of the 19th century, the Finnish people were already strongly nationalistic and were active across a broad front in various civic organisations and societies that envisioned Finland as a separate state.

The separatist route was also paved by positive signs on the economic front. The long period of peace, and in particular a sequence of significant social reforms introduced from the

1860s, led to flourishing industry and commerce, with markets found in both Russia and western Europe. The foodstuffs and pulp & paper industries were the most important economic motors in the latter half of the 19th century. Living standards rose rapidly and with them the population, which grew threefold in about a century. By the outbreak of World War One, Finland was home to nearly 3 million people.

Many Finns, from Ostrobothnia in particular, emigrated to North America and Australia in the late nineteenth century in search of a better life.

If the proximity of St. Petersburg was a huge boon in economic terms, it was rather more problematic from the perspective of security policy. As great-power politics became increasingly tense, Russia actively sought to dismantle the Finnish separatist "special relationship" in favour of something less privileged and autonomous, and the ensuing Russification process led to protests and a lengthy political dispute.

After Russia came out on the losing side of the Russo-Japanese War in 1905, the Tsar was obliged to submit to numerous reforms. In Finland this liberalisation led to the establishment in 1906 of a democratically-elected Parliament chosen by universal and equal suffrage. Finnish women were the first in Europe to be given full political rights.

Finland's annexation as part of Russia from 1809 had been one product of a major geopolitical chain reaction, and similar historical events led to the country's full independence in the latter stages of the First World War. Worn out with three years of fighting, Russia had slipped into internal strife and mayhem, and in the wake of the Bolsheviks' October Revolution, the Finnish Parliament proclaimed

AN INDEPENDENT REPUBLIC

the country independent on December 6th, 1917, on the basis of a proposal from the Senate.

However, with no formal authority in place to keep order, within a matter of months the fledgling republic had drifted into a short and violent civil war that was in practice a regional component of the broader chaos that was sweeping through Russia itself. By May 1918, the Finnish White faction, with the decisive support of troops from Germany, had won a complete victory over the socialist rebels, who had for their part received weapons from Soviet Russia.

The Russification that took place in the late nineteenth and early twentieth centuries is portrayed in Eetu Isto's painting *The Attack* (1899), in which the Maid of Finland is seen fighting to defend her autonomous rights against the double-headed eagle of Russia.

With Germany defeated in World War I, the original plans to make Finland a constitutional monarchy under a German king were scrapped in favour of a republican form of government and a constitution formulated in 1919. This document was to remain in force unchanged until 2000, when the previously wide-ranging powers of the President of the Republic were trimmed in favour of Parliament.

The first three decades of Finnish independence proved to be a painful rite of initiation for the young country. Economically speaking, Finland was thriving. Western Europe had largely replaced the old Russian markets, and Finnish cultural life underwent vibrant changes and won international recognition. The nation's political progress, on the other hand, was hampered by the legacies of the Civil War. The earlier wounds went untreated and the domestic political scene was starkly divided. By the beginning of the 1930s the anti-Communist tendencies of the radical right had reached a point where the entire parliamentary system came under threat. A failed rightist coup in 1932 was the high-water mark of this instability. However, by the spring of 1937 a broad-based majority government was formed, merging the political interests of the agrarian population and the working class, and in so doing creating the foundation for national consensus and the modern Finnish welfare state.

The period of stable and peaceful social progress was nevertheless short-lived. It was abruptly curtailed in the autumn of 1939 by the outbreak of the Second World War, and by demands from Moscow for territorial concessions by Finland. Once again, the closeness of St. Petersburg, or Leningrad as it was then known, was of paramount importance. When the Finns rejected the Soviet demands, the Red Army launched a large-scale attack on Finland from November 30th, 1939. The Finnish forces managed to halt the invasion. In terms of both men and materiel, the Red Army

The Civil War of 1918 ended in a victory parade in the Senate Square in which the troops were led by General G. Mannerheim. He later became commander of the Finnish forces during the Winter War of 1939–40 and the Continuation War of 1941–44. He served as President of the Republic from 1944 to 1946. In 2004 he was voted the greatest Finn of all time.

vastly outnumbered the Finnish troops, but the Finns were highly motivated, familiar with the terrain, and considerably better suited to fighting in extreme conditions – the winter of 1939–1940 was the coldest in living memory. The Finnish units exploited the forests and punished the cumbersome Russian motorized columns, surrounding and wiping out whole Soviet divisions. This conflict, the Winter War, lasted 105 days. In March 1940 the two sides signed a peace treaty. The Soviet Union feared that the Western Allies were about to intervene on behalf of the Finns, and Moscow was content at this stage to force some territorial concessions from Finland and the establishment of a Soviet military base on leased land in the Hanko Peninsula, south-west from Helsinki.

Independence was preserved, but the Winter War left a deep scar on the Finnish psyche. Finland's plight gained a great deal of sympathy in the western press, and Sweden provided material support in many forms, but militarily the Finns were left completely to their own devices. It was a stark and painful lesson. From then onwards, the Finnish political leadership and the great majority of the people understood that neither the Allied powers nor their Nordic neighbours would come to their aid if Finnish independence and sovereignty were the only assets at stake.

As a consequence of this understanding, President Risto Ryti and the army's commander-in-chief Gustaf Mannerheim quietly agreed to a German offer of military assistance in the winter of 1940–1941. Neither man held any great affection for the tenets of Nazi ideology, but both saw collaboration with Hitler's Germany as Finland's only means of salvation in the face of a new attempt on its borders by the Red Army. By June 1941, when the Germans launched Operation Barbarossa, the Finns were already fully mobilised and ready to attack. The Red Army launched bombing raids on several Finnish cities, allowing the Finnish government to describe Finland's countermeasures – taken a couple of weeks later – as a justified defensive response to Soviet aggression.

Finland never signed a formal political alliance with Nazi

Cultural life flourished in the 1920s and 1930s, with a new generation of writers, artists, and musicians who admired international trends and the romance of everything mechanical. Olavi Paavolainen and Mika Waltari, whose joint volume of poetry *Highways* (1928) reflected the spirit of the age, belonged to the nucleus of young writers known as The Torchbearers.

Germany, and the country had its own well-defined national objectives in the campaign known as the Continuation War (1941–1944) that followed. Nevertheless, in military terms this was patently a joint war against the Soviet Union. Germany had re-armed the Finnish forces, bore responsibility for much of the fighting on the front in northern Finland, and provided a significant part of the weaponry and raw materials required by the Finns throughout the duration of the common conflict.

In June 1944, when the Soviet Union began a massive artillery and infantry assault on the Karelian Isthmus in order to pressure Finland into suing for a separate peace agreement, air and ground support from Germany was instrumental in helping the Finns to stop the advancing Red Army at the critical moment. Shortly afterwards, the German armed forces found themselves under ever-increasing pressure from two directions following the Normandy landings, and this in turn opened the way to an armistice between Finland, the Soviet Union, and the Western Allies in September 1944. The terms of this truce were ratified in the Treaty of Paris of 1947. Once more, Finland had to agree to the surrender of substantial amounts of territory, and to the establishment of a large Soviet military base just west of the Finnish capital. In addition, the country was obliged to pay massive reparations to the Soviet Union and to bring the wartime government leaders to trial for criminal liability for the war.

Finland's position in Cold War Europe was exceptional in many respects. Unlike countries of eastern Europe, Finland was never occupied by the Red Army. In this way the country remained a western democracy, and – thanks to an astonishingly rapid process of industrialisation – by the 1970s Finland had achieved the same standard of living as western Europe. This made possible the creation of a welfare state along the lines of the Nordic model, accentuating social equality and civil rights. Then again, throughout the Cold War era Finland had to pay careful attention to the security interests of the Soviet Union.

In April 1948 Finland concluded a Treaty of Friendship, Cooperation and Mutual Assistance with the Soviet Union. This pact committed Finland to resist any armed attack against Finland, or against the Soviet Union through Finnish territory. The treaty remained in force until 1991 and decisively helped to sustain confidence-building and stability between the two countries, thereby laying the foundations for broad economic cooperation that naturally also contributed to Finnish development.

The darker side of this relationship with Moscow was that it did not always strengthen Western belief in the neutrality policy being actively pursued by the Finnish leadership. Nevertheless, during a quarter of a century in office (1956–1981) President Urho

Kekkonen gradually won international respect and recognition for his balancing act between East and West. The existence of a 1,300-kilometre land border with the USSR was a geographical reality that no amount of political rhetoric could change. In order that Finland should not have suffered too greatly from this, the country's export industries benefited from membership of EFTA (1961) and from a favourable free trade agreement with the EEC (1973).

In this way Finland quite cleverly managed to avoid conflicts with its powerful eastern neighbour while simultaneously becoming increasingly closely linked with the market economies of western Europe. In August 1975, thirty-five European and North American heads of state and government met in Helsinki to sign the Final Act of the Conference on Security and Cooperation in Europe. These "Helsinki Accords" were seen above all as a ratification of the post-

The Winter War (1939–40) lasted three and a half months, during which Finland repelled massive attacks by Soviet forces time after time. During this exceptionally cold winter, the enemy troops learned to fear Finnish ski patrols, which were likely to turn up without a sound where they were least expected.

war political division of Europe into East and West. At the same time, however, the Helsinki signatories agreed on common ground-rules on human rights issues, and political dissidents within the Socialist bloc seized eagerly upon these norms. The processes set in motion in Helsinki had a significant influence on the unravelling and eventual collapse of the Soviet empire in 1991.

Nobody in Finland, or for that matter anywhere else, had been able to envisage such an abrupt turn of events.

Even though the rate of growth was not as great as it had been in the 1960s and 70s, Finland continued to prosper through the 1980s. During the two presidential terms of Mauno Koivisto (1982–1994), Finnish governments – once a watchword in brevity and volatility – would consistently rule for a full four-year electoral term, bringing stability to the domestic politics of the nation of five million. New advances in information technology made their entrance. The state radio and television monopolies were gradually dismantled. Similar liberalisation was seen in the field of telephony, creating sound market conditions for the wired and wireless data communications revolutions of the 1990s.

As in many other countries, the freeing of international capital led in Finland to serious overheating in the national economy at the end of the 1980s. When this was accompanied closely by the collapse and disintegration of the Soviet Union, by a sharp decline in Finnish exports both to East and to West, and by less than competent monetary policies, the consequence was a deep economic depression between 1991 and 1994. Unemployment surged to a high of nearly 20% of the workforce. Entire branches of industry were wound up and state debts reached alarming levels, but the safety nets of the welfare state system withstood the strain and from 1995 onwards the country enjoyed a period of economic boom that extended into the new century. It may only be coincidence, but the nation's development curve closely matches that of Nokia, now a hugely successful global telecommunications player. At the beginning of the 1990s, this flagship of Finnish industry was in deep financial trouble after expanding beyond its means.

In the midst of the economic crisis, early in 1992, the Finnish government resolved to seek membership of the European Union. The decision was supported on both economic and security policy grounds. Within the Western community of nations a vision had emerged of a single market that would also have a common foreign and security policy. This seemed like a sensible idea in a country such as Finland, where there continued to be not unreasonable concerns about the developments going on within the new Russian Federation. Two years

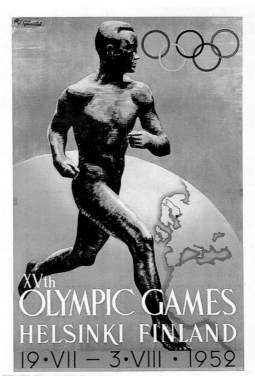

after the first approaches to Brussels, an agreement was reached on the terms of accession. In a consultative referendum held in October 1994, nearly 57% of Finns were in favour of membership. Finland duly joined the EU along with Austria and Sweden on January 1st, 1995.

In the early stages, EU membership was seen as extremely important for the Finnish identity, which has always had a strong penchant for close ties with the west European camp and Western civilisation as a whole. This fact became obvious in 1998, when Parliament voted in favour of Finnish espousal of European economic and monetary union, and the adoption of the euro. Later, in the autumn of 1999, when Finland held the rotating six-month Presidency of the European Council for the first time, there was again a sense of that early enthusiastic zeal for the Union.

The Helsinki Olympic Games of 1952 marked the beginning of a new era for Finland: the war reparations had just been paid off, Armi Kuusela had been voted Miss Universe, and now the Olympics were focusing the attention of the whole world on this small country.

Thereafter the enthusiasm has clearly waned, even though Finland numbers among those EU member states that have benefited most from membership, economically and in the sphere of security policy.

There have been a number of causes for this cooling towards the European Union and its structures.

X10370

X10370064188

At the beginning of the current decade the EU member states performed sluggishly on the economic front, and the notable wave of enlargement eastwards from May 2004 brought new problems to the surface and to the negotiating table. A more significant reason for the somewhat indifferent approach to the Union among everyday Finns is nevertheless the rapid changes witnessed in the global economy and in data communications. The European Union is and will hopefully continue to be a common home for Europeans. And yet it is now increasingly easy to transfer oneself in words, sounds, and images – and naturally also physically by air – to other continents and to experience a wider world beyond Europe's shores.

In a country such as Finland, which has often shown an almost childlike fascination with technology and communications, this tendency may be particularly strong. Whatever the truth of this, as we approach the second decade of the new millennium, Finland seems to be coping quite well with the accelerating pace of changes going on around it.

One of the earliest maps to depict Finland and its culture in detail was the *Carta Marina* of Olaus Magnus, printed in Venice in 1539. Based on extensive fieldwork and a study of classical sources such as the writings of Tacitus, it remained the main source for all maps of northern Europe until well into the seventeenth century. One of the most recent printed representations of Finland, and the most widely distributed, is on euro banknotes.

Henrik Meinander, Ph.D., is professor of history at the University of Helsinki and head of its Department of History.

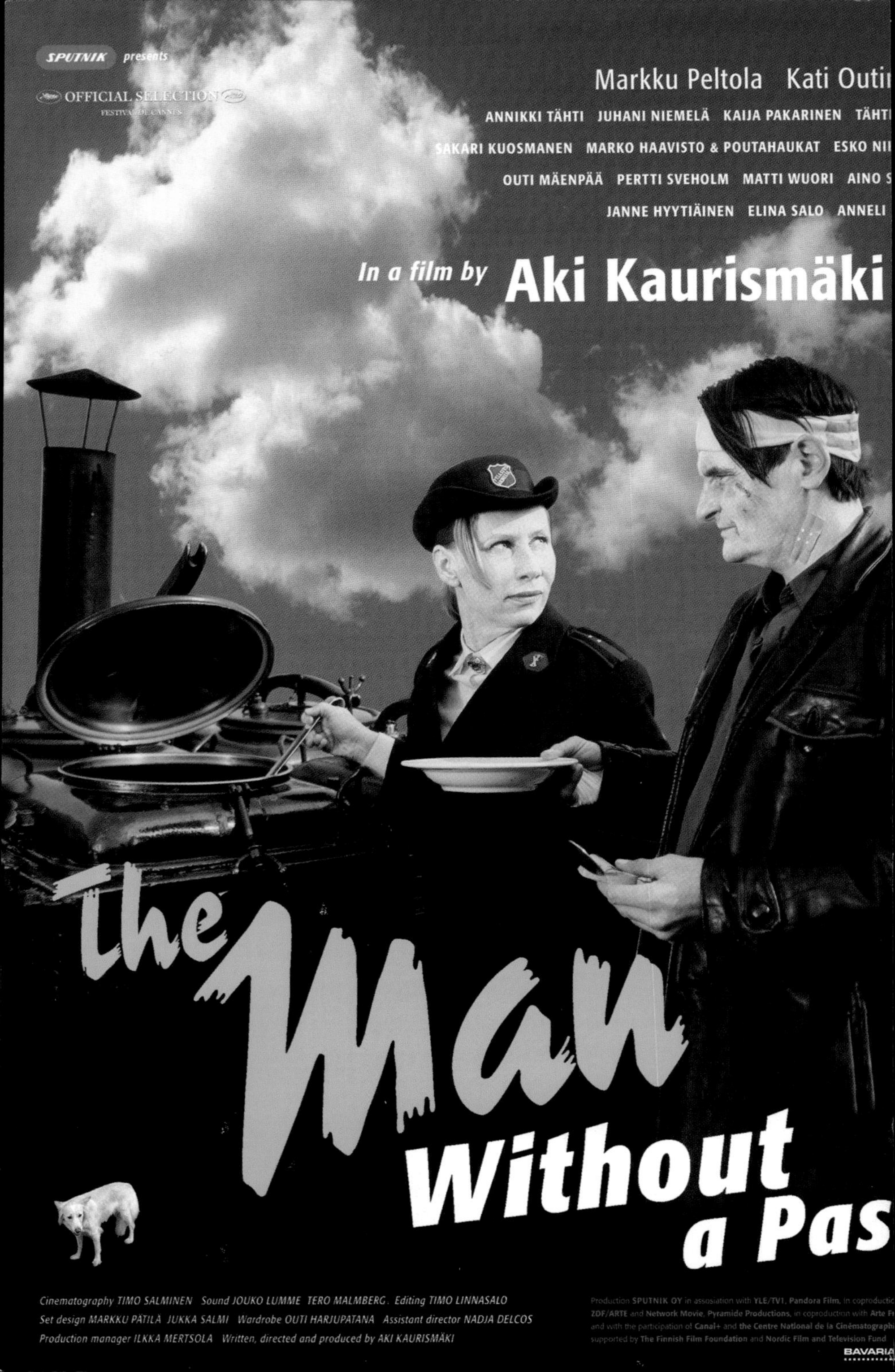

SPUTNIK presents
OFFICIAL SELECTION
Markku Peltola
ANNIKKI TÄHTI JUHANI NIEMELÄ KAIJA PAKARINEN
SAKARI KUOSMANEN MARKO HAAVISTO & POUTAHAUKAT
OUTI MÄENPÄÄ PERTTI SVEHOLM MATTI WUORI
JANNE HYYTIÄINEN ELINA SALO ANNELI
In a film by Aki Kaurismäki
The Man Without a
Cinematography TIMO SALMINEN Sound JOUKO LUMME TERO MALMBERG. Editing TIMO LINNASALO
Set design MARKKU PÄTILÄ JUKKA SALMI Wardrobe OUTI HARJUPATANA Assistant director NADJA DELCOS
Production manager ILKKA MERTSOLA Written, directed and produced by AKI KAURISMÄKI
Production SPUTNIK OY in assosiation with YLE/TV1, Pandora Film, in
ZDF/ARTE and Network Movie, Pyramide Productions, in coproduction with Arte
and with the participation of Canal+ and the Centre National de la
supported by The Finnish Film Foundation and Nordic Film and Television Fund

2

Lifestyle, Culture and Mentality

Rural and urban areas are force fields shaping collective memories. National identity was grounded in the agrarian ideal, nature, the symbolism of the forests and the romanticism of the Kalevala. Urbanization came later and faster than anywhere else in Europe, beginning only in the 1960s. The lifestyle is Scandinavian.

The Kaurismäki brothers are well known for their films in which the dialogue is reduced to a minimum. Aki Kaurismäki's The Man Without a Past is poised on an indeterminate boundary between laughter and grief.

What does it mean to be a Finn? One can speak of a Finnish identity in terms of both history and geography. In its human geography Finland has a pronounced dual identity, as an outpost of Western Europe or the most western of the countries of Eastern Europe. The Finns developed into nationhood in the borderlands between Sweden and Russia, and their history has been greatly influenced by their location as neighbours of two major powers in Northern Europe. The political concepts of north, west and east can help us to place Finland within the world, for it has been affected by all the wars and crises, social upheavals and revolutions that have been a part of Europe's history. The peacetime identity of the Finnish people has been a narrative of growth, the seeking and finding of a cultural and social ethos of their own, but at times of war they have found themselves occupying a border territory and performing a tenuous balancing act in matters of power politics.

The painters Albert Edelfelt and Akseli Gallen-Kallela were even moved to defy the ravages of winter and put on their fur coats in order to paint the winter landscape as seen from the hilltop at Koli in Karelia. Eero Järnefelt immortalized the scenery of Lake Pielinen in its autumn colours. This area, protected as a national park, has remained virtually unchanged over the centuries.

The image of the country, the nation and a national culture centred on the Finnish language was created in the nineteenth century, when Finland was part of the Russian Empire. Like the other minority nationalities within that empire, the Finns were united

by their ethnic background, language and origins. The process of nation building was one of identification with the common people. Finnish nationalism was based on the possession of a national language and culture and the existence of a strong state organization and network of provinces, which meant that Finland already resembled a Scandinavian country constitutionally, administratively and in terms of its population structure. Its social and democratic foundation had grown up from the independent, landowning peasant class. Even during the "Russian period" the people became accustomed

to defending their own institutions, cautiously but resolutely – a feature that still applies to political discussion to this day. Thus relations with Russia or the Soviet Union have continued to be a matter of crucial importance even after the gaining of independence in 1917, and every alteration in these relations has led to a political reassessment of the country's self-image.

The Finnish flag, adopted in 1918, features a cross, alluding to the ancient, symbolic Nordic tradition of state, church and flag. Christian, and especially Evangelical-Lutheran, traditions have bound Finland to the other Nordic countries for centuries, and many features of the Finnish character and way of life can still be attributed to these, including the people's intense devotion to a culture of hard work and the value placed on a simple way of life and a personal relationship with God. These features are often regarded very highly in comparisons between southern and northern European mentalities, and in this respect the Finnish image is still shaped by the country's links with Sweden and the Swedish language, which remains Finland's second official language. Six hundred years of joint history with Sweden have left an indelible mark on its governmental, political and institutional characteristics, and relations with that country, where there are now hundreds of thousands of people of Finnish descent, still exist on many levels and are of the utmost importance.

The Finns look on themselves as living in a "small country",

When National Romanticism reached Finland in the late nineteenth century it gave rise to a wealth of artists and composers inspired by "the common people" and unspoiled nature. Eastern Karelia, plus the hill country of north-eastern Finland, and forests and lakes in general, became symbolic features of the fatherland.

33

It calls for a measure of courage to go swimming through a hole in the ice of a lake, but tens of thousands of Finns can't be wrong: winter swimming is good for you.

for in spite of its vast area, it has remarkably few inhabitants, only about five million, and they are well aware of speaking a rare language. They are still apt to speak of their "Finnish identity" in very general terms, and are curious to know what others think of their country. The national ideology and the people's trust in the public sector administration continue to manifest themselves even in the views of the younger generation.

When outsiders speak of Finland, however, it is difficult to find any consistent interpretation. It is often regarded as a distant, cold and mystical country where the people are of a fair complexion and remain silent fluently in two languages. The Finnish speakers are of Finno-Ugric origin, and their language resembles Hungarian. They are mad on sport and sauna, and they have formed their views on existence over a long period of time and are reluctant to give them up.

The Finns are accustomed to discussing their "national identity" as if it were an immutable fact of life, although in practice it is difficult nowadays to find a common denominator among this group of just over five million people who are obliged to respond to the challenges of globalization and a multicultural world in just the same way as the rest of Europe. The Finns themselves prefer to talk about nature and their relations with the forests, the sea, the islands, the lakes, the fells of Lapland and green values in general. They have experienced a rapid process of urbanization since 1945, but they still see themselves as close to the countryside and an agrarian way of life. The welfare state is a matter of great importance to them, and they speak with enthusiasm about the significance of education, equality of the sexes and the crucial role of the public sector in the distribution of affluence.

Finland has altered dramatically in a hundred years, and this is clearly to be seen in the landscape. There are few signs left of the predominantly agrarian society of a hundred years ago, when the majority of the people were tenant farmers living in simple cottages. The tale of the Finnish identity is very much that of the development that took place during the twentieth century, the long road to education, freedom from poverty, and urbanization through increased social mobility. The whole century was a time of seeking political and social means of removing class distinctions in order to achieve a free, democratic and egalitarian society based on high levels of education and intellectual achievement, justice, communality and collective responsibility. The direction has been similar in most other European countries, but the exceptional things about the trend in Finland have been the speed of the change and the spirit of consensus regarding its political aims. Each generation has had to adapt anew to the constantly changing conditions. The Finns have been on the move: from the rural areas to the towns and cities, from impoverishment to affluence, to jobs and an improved social status though education.

The light summer nights tempt people to stay out of doors for as long as possible.

These trends have raised Helsinki, which became the capital only in 1812, to the status of a major growth centre. Unlike many European capitals, it has a city centre that was planned for this purpose. The Classical style of architecture, adopted at the Tsar's behest, was intended to symbolize its new status as a garrison town, administrative centre and manifestation of the might of the Russian

Empire. The chief buildings required for the exercise of power were arranged around the Senate Square: the Senate building itself, representing political power, the Church of St. Nicholas, representing spiritual power, and the main building of the University, the cradle of intellectual power. Thus the square became a metaphor for "the course of history and historical events". Subsequent collective memories associated with it do indeed tell of the creation of the Finnish state, the construction of a national identity and the formation of a civic society. It is undoubtedly the most fundamentally urban of all sights in Finland, a monumental, light-coloured, consistent Empire-style façade that opens out towards the sea. This view of the capital city has risen to be a symbol for the whole country and nation.

There were still only 7.5% town dwellers among the Finns in the year 1900, and the whole process of urbanization took place very late, mostly at a rapid pace after 1945. The accompanying social upheavals nevertheless drew attention to the problems of urban life, and discussions were for a long time coloured by a fear of towns. The modern Finnish identity has arisen through an interaction between two spheres of life, rural and urban, in which the course of history has played a major part. The national image was originally associated with the way of life of a peasant farmer, a provincial orientation and the desire to take enlightenment and education to the people. Political cohesion in internal affairs was ensured for

Living conditions have changed dramatically over the last 100 years. The ideal of "a cottage of one's own and a potato patch" was still a feature of everyday life in the 1950s. Then began the great migration to the towns.

decades by the parallel existence of a powerful state administration and a rural hinterland, a pattern that received support from the idealization of the agrarian way of life, the symbolism attached to nature and the forests and the National Romanticism embodied in the *Kalevala*, the national epic poem.

The resolution of the status of the tenant farmers in 1922 and the re-housing of persons displaced by the war in 1945 were both events that served to prolong the period of predominantly rural settlement and promote agrarian values, but it was finally the great restructuring of society in the 1960s that caused hundreds of thousands of small farmers to move south to seek work in the towns. The resulting process of urbanization was one of the fastest and longest delayed in Europe, which means that the first thoroughly urbanized generations of Finns reached adulthood only from the 1980s onwards, generations educated in the new comprehensive schools and taking their values from the global popular culture. The migration to the towns is still

This family portrait was taken in the 1920s. The children and grandchildren will probably have had some formal education and ended up as town-dwellers.

continuing, however, thrusting more people into the sphere of the urban way of life.

Although the typical urban landscape for most of these people is the suburb, on the border where the town meets the forest, the problem of "the flight from the countryside" is still an urgent topic of public discussion. It has taken a long time for the urban image to be incorporated into the national identity, for it was only the revolution in culture and values, the rise in the standard of living and the migration of population experienced in the 1960s that made room for an urban ethos. The new ideology laid more emphasis on the modern, individualist way of life, cultural mobility, rationality, pluralism, international thinking, equality, democracy and the importance of education. The process of social change took time, but it was the cultural revolution of the 1960s that made it possible to break away from the traditional institutions and agrarian-based cultural uniformity. The integration into Europe represented by the step of joining the EU in 1995 then served to underline the role of the cities, in particular, in an entirely new way and to seal the victory of the urban culture and way of life. Themes of multicultural tolerance and understanding permeated public discussion, effectively diluting the former national cultural uniformity in the course of time.

In spite of the rapid social changes, the Finnish identity has remained firmly anchored in the countryside. Much importance is attached to regional development, as reflected in the powerful network of provincial universities and colleges of higher education, and many of the salient features of the rural culture may still be perceived in people's thinking and predilections. Finland was a land of small farmers up to the 1960s, and the farming population contributed greatly to the emerging working class and the various categories of white collar employees. People have been recruited from the countryside for work in factories, service occupations, administration, the media and education, and the result is that a certain rural nostalgia lives on everywhere. It may

THE FINNISH SAUNA

Although increasing numbers of urban dwellings have a sauna, the pleasure of washing oneself in a sauna is above all something that is associated with the countryside and one's summer cottage. The heating of the sauna is "a man's job": felling the trees, chopping the firewood, carrying the water and lighting the stove. Small children usually go to sauna with their parents, and people take a relaxed and natural view of nakedness in this context. There are many kinds and sizes of sauna, of course, but the basic model has a single

A Finn could not live without a sauna. The age-old sauna customs have scarcely altered at all, even though many town houses have an electric stove instead of the traditional wood-fired one. Pekka Halonen, *Sauna* (1925).

stove that heats the space to about 80°C beforehand, a separate washing room and possibly a sitting room with an open hearth. Many cottages have a traditional "smoke sauna", which has no chimney and has to be heated for several hours, so that the smoke accumulates in the room and is then allowed out through a vent before the sauna begins. The bathers in a sauna sit on high benches to enjoy the heat and can throw water onto the stones on the top of the stove to release more moisture. They then go out to wash and perhaps swim. All this makes one hungry and thirsty, of course, and sauna beer or some other refreshing drink is part of the ritual, as is the eating of sausage (often cooked in a metal dish on the top of the stove). Sauna is a form of both inner and outer cleansing for most Finns and an essential part of their weekend.

be seen in the arts, in literature and in the cinema, so that the most successful works are those that depict the great social upheavals themselves, the time when pioneer settlers built a home and tended the fields with their own hands, the migrations into the towns, sufferings during the war and the prospects for returning to the idyllic countryside. It is only relatively recently that Finnish art, films and literature have discovered urban areas and their way of life.

On the other hand, this is a modern post-industrial country with a high level of investment in modern technology that lays much store by the opportunities offered in that sphere. The industrial revolution has also been part of the "great narrative", and Finland is often referred to as a country led by its engineers. The forest industries linked the country to the world economy way back in the seventeenth century, and from that time onwards it was through technical advances that affluence was achieved and standards of living improved. The importance of the forests is still very much in evidence in the structure of Finnish industry, where the "green gold" continues to play a key role. The forests represent a source of industrial raw materials and employment, welfare and security, trade and prosperity. They have provided material well-being for industrialists, lumbermen, papermakers and log floaters alike, and they have also been of considerable geopolitical importance. Finally, they have been, and continue to be, a rich source of creative inspiration and a place for relaxation.

Apart from the fact that a large proportion of the Finnish people own forests and are interested in their management, there is a lively culture of summer cottages and holiday villas, which provides many people with a lifeline to the countryside. There are some 400,000 second homes in Finland, mostly on

the sea shore or beside a lake, in Kuusamo or in Lapland, and an increasing number are nowadays habitable during the winter as well, so that people can spend a large amount of time there at weekends in winter and in summer. It is also becoming more and more common for people to acquire such a cottage in their parents' or grandparents' home district. In many ways the summer cottage is a Finn's real location, for the connection with nature, peace and quiet and certain types of landscape form the nucleus of his mental constitution, and the cycle of the seasons plays a major part in this, too.

The countryside of old lives on in people's memories even today, even though it has nowadays become urbanized, too, and farming has undergone vast structural changes of its own. The

About half a million second homes includes everything from modest cabins to well-appointed villas. A little red-painted cottage on a lake shore represents the typical Finnish landscape of the imagination – a place where sublime peace reigns through all seasons of the year. In summer there is the sauna under birch trees on the shore, and in the winter you can have your own private ski trail across the lake.

first novel to be published in Finnish, Aleksis Kivi's The *Seven Brothers* (1870), describes the traditional agrarian society at a time when it was still untouched by the ways of the world. The orphaned brothers represent the great narrative of how early primitive communities were brought to heel by the desire to achieve progress and become educated, although they remain ordinary people who are ready to rise up in revolt against the fine gentlemen of society. Kivi's tale has become a basic national legend, and although the Finns no longer emulate the wildness of the seven brothers, they still retain a closeness to nature that has replaced agrarian values. The more they have become urbanised, the more they have developed a clearer bond with the forests and the values represented in them. Even an IT professional operating in the global market will remember to point out the importance of the forests for creativity and nonconformity.

The landscape is a relatively clear, accepted national symbol, the connection between patriotism and a relationship with nature that was established in Finland and Scandinavia in the nineteenth century. The everyday forest landscape became a symbol of one's home district and fatherland and was linked with a sense of the continuity of this national affiliation. Thus the essentially chaotic, wild, unknown forest was transformed into a symbol for the community, a landscape for use in art and advertising and a design feature for coins and banknotes, a national landscape, in effect. The art and industrial arts of the modern nation were committed to preserving and promoting this image of the people and nature. Thus the works of the golden age of national art, around the end of the nineteenth century and beginning of the twentieth, depict the people as living unpretentiously in a smokehouse, or standing in their yard or outside a church, cultivating clearings burned in the forest, or seeking education for themselves. Landscapes also play an important part in the present-day national anthem, *Maamme* (Our Land, 1848, F. Pacius – J. L. Runeberg), in which an inland scene with a lake and stretch of forest opening out obliquely upwards is looked on as the intrinsic image of Finnish identity. Other visions are perhaps more dramatic or austere scenes of forests, rapids, hills or winter landscapes. The paintings and frescoes that have been produced to illustrate the *Kalevala*, first published in 1835, represent the same range of landscape features perceived as national, and nowadays the concept of a "national landscape" has been made official with the declaration of an accepted list of such views, including landscapes in a natural state, "cultural landscapes" of rural areas under cultivation and pictures of historical monuments. In other words, a national landscape is an image of Finland of a kind which the visitor to the country can be expected to encounter repeatedly.

The Finns celebrate Independence Day on 6th December, the date on which Parliament approved the country's declaration of independence in 1917. Over time, and particularly since 1945, it has come to be celebrated by all sectors of society, with particular attention to those groups and individuals who were most closely engaged in the struggle for independence. Thus the students, the defence forces and, of course, the President are most prominent. The blue and white colours of the Finnish flag are to be seen everywhere, on television screens, in shop windows and in the two lighted candles that many families place in the windows of their homes. Held on a dark and frequently cold winter's day, it is a solemn, dignified observance which has only very recently taken on a lighter tone, with some carnival elements added to it. Students walk in procession to war graves carrying flaming torches, and a splendid reception is held at the Presidential Palace and relayed live to the nation on television.

The history of Finland as an independent state thus goes back less than a hundred years, and the constitutional process of establishing the country was bound up with a bitter Civil War between the Reds, representing mainly the urban working class and the poorer elements in the rural population, and the Whites that cast a shadow over the definitions of the nation, the state and national unanimity for a long time. It took years for people to reconcile themselves with the circumstances of this upheaval, and to some extent the process is still going on. One immediate outcome, however, was that one part of the population was left on the sidelines in the aftermath and labelled "unpatriotic". Political integration was really achieved only in the 1960s. Issues arising from the Civil War and interpretations of them have also been bound up, inextricably and controversially, with class distinctions in society and with relations with Russia or the Soviet Union. Each generation has had to determine its own attitude towards the circumstances that led to war, what happened in the war itself, the consequences of the war and Finland's internal and external relations in general.

The twentieth century as a whole was a period marked by certain outstanding years and certain outstanding public and

political figures. In addition to independence, every generation has had its own way of commemorating the achievement of universal suffrage in 1906 and the two separate wars waged against the Soviet Union, the Winter War of 1939–1940 and the Continuation War of 1941–1944, in which the Finns held out heroically for a long time but eventually joined the ranks of the defeated nations. The war period introduced many features into the Finns' self-image, including some that acquired mythical proportions. Reports of the courage shown by the Finnish forces spread throughout the world via war correspondents, and volunteers came from Sweden and many other countries to fight alongside the Finns. Meanwhile, thousands of Finnish children were being evacuated to Sweden for safety. The spirit of the Winter War was at its best a

On Independence Day, December 6, students in Helsinki march in procession with flaming torches from the tombs of heroes in Hietaniemi to the Senate Square.

huge, collective commitment to a single overwhelming objective. The mobilization of reserves from all walks of life increased the spirit of national unity, and the working class willingly joined in the defence of their country.

One notable feature of the Finnish war effort was that every attempt was made to bring the fallen in battle back for burial in war graves in their own local cemeteries, watched over by a monument erected in their honour as heroes. Since then visits of remembrance to these war graves have become a part of the normal patriotic Independence Day observances of war veterans and students alike. As in all wars, families lost fathers, husbands and sons in action, and the personal grief of such families served to unite mothers, war widows and orphans with their counterparts in other countries. War experiences have been preserved in the collective memory through literature, memoirs, plays, films and historical works, and the sprig of oak leaves on the badge worn by war veterans has become a symbol of the national spirit of independence. Finland and its capital were never occupied during the war, and the country

succeeded in preserving its political sovereignty.

It has been the custom to dedicate days of celebration to various outstanding national figures: statesmen, politicians, soldiers and other key members of society including representatives of the arts. The oldest stratum of such figures contains the creators of the intellectual foundations of the new nation: Porthan, Snellman, Runeberg, Topelius, Minna Canth and Aleksis Kivi, followed by military leaders, above all G.Mannerheim, Marshal of Finland, statesmen who led the country through critical stages in its history, such as Presidents Risto Ryti, J. K. Paasikivi and Urho Kekkonen, and internationally acknowledged artistic giants such as Eliel Saarinen, Jean Sibelius and Alvar Aalto. These acts of commemoration and the raising of statues have also extended to sports personalities, past and present, among them the runner Paavo Nurmi and the Formula One racing driver Mika Häkkinen. Moreover, the homes of national figures have been opened to the public, the oldest of these being the Runeberg Museum in Porvoo and the Mannerheim Museum in Helsinki.

Sport has given the nation many heroes. One outstanding area of success has been motor sport, particularly rally driving and the Formula 1 Grand Prix circuit. The Finnish winners of the Formula 1 world championship to date have been Kimi Räikkönen (2007), Mika Häkkinen (1998, 1999) and Keke Rosberg (1983), whose son Nico Rosberg is one of the new rising stars of the sport.

The fundamental notion behind Finnish nationalism from the beginning was that the strength of this small nation was to lie in education and culture, and there have been two "golden ages" in the country's history when forms of artistic expression, particularly painting, literature, industrial art, design and architecture, combined to create a sense of Finnish originality. The two movements involved were the National Romantic era of the late nineteenth century and the age of modern Functionalism. The aim in these periods was clearly to develop forms of art that corresponded to the "spirit of the times" by adapting models taken from elsewhere to Finnish conditions. Streamlined form, authenticity, economy, practicality, unpretentiousness and "noble simplicity" together with motifs derived from vegetation and nature in general have become typical features of Finnish design. Politically, architecture was harnessed for the purpose of building a new society, so that the National Romanticism of the nineteenth century may be said

Much of modern Finnish design sets out from simple ideas and natural materials. The classics of the 1950's and 1960's mingle perfectly with the contemporary style and mindset. Even the most traditional article of all times, the Finnish musical instrument the *kantele* (on the bench), has renewed its looks with the ultramodern styling of the Wing kantele.

to have reflected the goal of statehood and Functionalism the ideal of the modern, international, democratic welfare state of the twentieth century.

Finland was quite literally built in the twentieth century, and since its buildings are among the youngest in Europe, it has naturally become a model country for modern architecture. The concept of *Finnish Design*, on the other hand, emerged after 1945, when Finnish artists won a succession of international design awards with ideas that reflected the optimism and building boom of the post-war reconstruction period. There was a demand for new home interiors, and designers were able to create innovative, elegant everyday articles and utensils. Architecture and design have been perceived to an exceptional extent as heroic artistic achievements and culturally significant export commodities, so that their products have been held up as symbols of the modern Finnish society. The figurehead of this movement was undoubtedly Alvar Aalto (1898–1976), whose works became the national heritage of "Republican Finland", as he skilfully combined international elements with the ideals of Functionalism and the use of both Finnish and exotic materials: glass, wood, plywood, brick and marble. The same national status was achieved in the clothing and textiles of the *Marimekko* company with its young designers.

The exceptional features of nature in the north have always been a source of inspiration for artists. Design objects, jewellery and textiles emulating the forms of plants, water and ice capture the variations in light and shade. Much of the modern Finnish design sets out from simple ideas and natural materials. The curves of Alvar Aalto's world-famous *Savoy* vase and the *Planetary Valleys* necklace created by Björn Weckström for Princess Leia in the film *Star Wars* are Finnish classics.

Art and music clearly represent "national" projects in the Finnish historical context. The "golden age" at the end of the nineteenth and beginning of the twentieth century was followed by a period when national expectations were high. From 1917 onwards painting and sculpture were harnessed for the purpose of constructing a homespun cultural history for the young country, although in practice they lagged behind somewhat in the modernization race by comparison with architecture, and it was

only in the 1950s and 1960s that modernism and abstract art began to transform the world of visual values. Music, on the other hand, has succeeded in maintaining the prominent role that it occupied while it was involved in the cultural and ideological shaping of the new nation-state. Jean Sibelius (1865–1957) had become a national monument during his own lifetime, his compositions expressing values still revered to this day, and he overshadowed the musical achievements of most of his contemporaries. It was only in the 1950s that modernist composition techniques began to distance themselves from the style recognised as nationalist, whereupon the *avant garde* of the 1960s was welcomed with enthusiasm. Music is now one of Finland's best exports and upholds a Finnish presence in the world at large.

Folk music, choral music, opera and light music all have a place of their own in the Finnish narrative. An interest in folk music can be a manifestation of interest in one's roots and in the preservation of vernacular musical values, while choral music has clearly acquired a patriotic flavour, especially as practised in student circles. The elevation of the song *Maamme* (Our Land) to the status of national anthem took place on the strength of an impressive first performance at a student celebration in 1848, its repeated use at academic functions and in schools, and its inclusion in the programmes of provincial celebrations and song festivals. Choral singing became a mixture of song, politics, ideology and linguistic loyalties, and that being so it continues to this day

to give expression to a whole complex of patriotic feelings. The opera boom is of far more recent origin, being connected with the rise in popularity of classical music in the 1970s and the success enjoyed by the Finnish operatic composers Aulis Sallinen and Joonas Kokkonen. The success of Finnish opera productions at home and abroad was skilfully exploited to boost plans to build a new National Opera House in Helsinki. This was completed in 1993, to the joint satisfaction of composers, librettists, conductors and singers alike, not to mention the National Ballet, for which it meant a substantial improvement in performance facilities.

The early days of Finnish theatre were similarly connected with the nationalist awakening, and again interest grew "from the bottom up". Amateur theatrical, poetry-reading and play-reading circles were formed in various parts of the country, by both linguistic groups, Finnish-speaking and Swedish-speaking, in conjunction with the general rise of civic organizations. Performances were held in makeshift theatres, workers' institutes, temperance societies and youth clubs, in schools and at student gatherings. The first professional theatres were opened in the 19th century in Turku, Viipuri and Helsinki. Finnish plays are still extremely popular, and the theatre continues to be regarded – in the spirit of the radicalism of the 1960s – as a form of culture intended to express opinions on matters of public concern. Finnish films have relocated from the countryside to the towns in recent years and have achieved something of an international reputation, mainly thanks to the

The best-known Finnish cultural figures internationally are composers, conductors, musicians and dancers. Recent successes have included the composers Kaija Saariaho and Magnus Lindberg and the conductor Esa-Pekka Salonen. Acts that have prospered on the rock scene include The Rasmus, HIM and the Eurovision Song Contest winners Lordi, and in contemporary dance Tero Saarinen.

The beloved Moomin characters created by the artist and author Tove Jansson first conquered the world through the original children's books and then through strip cartoons and animated films. The soft, cuddly, philosophical Moomin family were commemorated with their very own fluffy-surfaced postage stamp in 2004.

down-to-earth, highly personal and minimalist flavour with a more or less universal message from directors Aki Kaurismäki and his brother Mika.

Finns have a great respect for literature in all its forms and reading in general. The badge of academia, the lyre and wreath, is deeply embedded in popular symbolism, backed by the value placed upon books, reading, libraries, education, schools and study and their popularity among all strata of society. Finnish literature began as national literature, aimed at building a national identity, modelling this function on the older tradition of Swedish literature, and it did indeed succeed in creating a truly Finnish tradition – the shaping of a national persona through parallel linguistic and aesthetic development. Even as society became more cynical and more modern, opening itself up to international influences, literature retained its purer sense of mission. Authors continue to be Finnish in their writing and to write about being Finnish, for although the archetypes, the pioneer settler clearing his own land and the peasant farmer, have become more urbanized, the basic message remains the same. What recent literature has in common with that of earlier times is that it portrays itself often with an element of parody. The successful, widely read authors, in Finnish and in Swedish, enjoy a high degree of popularity among ordinary people throughout the country.

One important factor behind the vitality of cultural life has been an interaction that collectively involves government cultural policy, local authority education policy, private artistic activity and popular interest. Local authorities took an interest in promoting culture at various levels, and cultural and educational policy played an important role when a process of renewal began within society. The major reforms of the school system and universities in the 1970s and 1980s had one concrete aim above all else: to increase social equality. Life-long learning became a national objective and led many people to adult education centres in search of supplementary courses and re-training. And the same objective was pursued elsewhere, as the arts, sport and other leisure activities were all regarded as services to be provided by the welfare state, with particular attention to marginal groups such as children, the elderly, the disabled and minorities. The government set up an administration to organise and support various types of artistic expression, increased public funding on the arts and took steps to stimulate local and regional cultural activities.

The underlying principle in this "peaceful cultural revolution" was the desire to activate people intellectually and physically, to spread cultural facilities throughout the country and to achieve an egalitarian distribution of opportunities for self-improvement. This process left its monuments in towns and villages, in the form of new local institutions such as theatres and concert halls, orchestras and museums. New libraries, multipurpose buildings, art galleries, schools of music, sports arenas, ice rinks and swimming pools were built all over the country from the late 1960s onwards, often designed by the best architects of the day. Contrary to the situation in many other countries, the word "culture" still has a positive ring about it in Finland.

Among the indicators of a strong cultural spirit straddling the boundary between public and private enterprise are the innumerable cultural festivals and other village or suburban fêtes and celebrations that take place in summertime all over the country. From this plenitude of local events have emerged a number of high quality summer festivals, each reflecting strongly the profile of its particular locality. Some places have concentrated on developing

The action-packed world of dogs conjured up by the graphic artist and writer Mauri Kunnas introduces children to facts of Finnish history, literature and folklore in a cleverly amusing fashion.

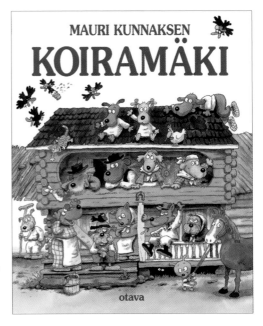

MAURI KUNNAKSEN

KOIRAMÄKI

otava

Helsinki has a reputation for its top-class night life, with innumerable bars, clubs and festivals featuring world-class performers and providing highly professional entertainments. one branch of art and in so doing have created a reputation for themselves nationally and internationally. Good examples of this development are the Savonlinna Opera Festival, the Kaustinen Folk Music Festival, and the chamber music festivals at Kuhmo, Naantali and Korsholm. Similarly, the Tango Festival at Seinäjoki, the Ruissalo Rock Festival and the Pori Jazz Festival are all fine exponents of their genre. There are many other smaller venues, including Sysmä, Kangasniemi, Porvoo, Inkoo, Joroinen and Viitasaari, where music and other forms of art are staged in an improvised fashion in churches, manor houses, dance pavilions, barns and other farm buildings, or even old factory premises.

WOMEN IN SOCIETY

The political foundation for the identity of Finnish women lies in their awareness that they were the first in Europe to gain full voting rights. That was in the parliamentary elections of 1906. Their advance towards fully equal status with men has also been influenced by the opening of all paths of education to them and by the custom of both sexes going out to work. The assumption that

Finnish women will be in full-time employment reflects the basic structure of the erstwhile agrarian society, in which participation by both sexes was required to ensure a regular income in all social strata. Culturally, this has led to the image of the strong working woman, fairly independent in her own sphere of activity, who lives and works alongside her husband, be they country folk or living in a town. As an alternative to marriage and raising a family, many educated working women prefer to live on their own.

The suffragism typical of the industrialised countries of Europe never really caught on in Finland, as the relationship between the sexes developed naturally into one of reciprocal companionship as social development advanced. This companionship ensured the integration of both partners as political and cultural actors on an equal footing. Education became available to women at an early stage, and Finland has a long tradition of girls' schools. Education and school attendance have provided both sexes with individualized means of improving the external and internal circumstances of their own lives, and wartime conditions finally opened up the universities, colleges and schools to women in an unprecedented fashion, since when the generations of female students have more than held their own. Women are also enthusiastic consumers of all aspects of culture.

The development of the welfare state from 1945 onwards was to a very considerable extent a "women's project". Discussion of the role of the

This promised land of cultural festivals is graced by more than 2000 summertime events devoted to music, literature, dance and other art forms. The Seinäjoki Tango Market is one that is constantly growing in popularity.

Elovena

The prototypical Finnish female is a nostalgic legacy from the agrarian age. She is blue-eyed, rosy-cheeked and has long blonde plaits. This is still the epitome of womanhood for many people.

sexes in the 1960s laid emphasis on the Nordic model, which aimed to eliminate a woman's dependence on her husband for her upkeep, to improve educational opportunities, to encourage employment outside the home and to increase the provision of children's day care and other family and social welfare services. It was the government that emerged at this point as "the woman's best friend", by guaranteeing political approval for these social reforms. It was a period of far-reaching change in the status of women and of the family. The entry of women into the working community added to their visibility in politics, administration, tertiary education and the media, and it was during those years that the current model for the role of women in society evolved. The ideal was to be able to combine a job and a family, and it led in time to the incorporation of the principle of equality of the sexes into social institutions, political programmes and welfare reforms. But in spite of all the aforementioned progress, equality in pay has not yet been achieved.

Stereotypes for Finnish women are to be found in the arts. The Maid of Finland, rustic, pure, and clad in national costume, became established as a symbol of Finnishness in the nineteenth century, as did the female figures in the *Kalevala*, Aino, Kyllikki, Louhi and the Mistress of Pohjola, all strong, resilient characters. The hard-working mother figure of immense moral strength emerged during the golden age of the national literature, so that as the male characters gradually became more degenerate, the females gained in stature and credibility. The Finnish woman as portrayed in artistic contexts is a rural wife and mother, diligent, unyielding in the struggle for survival, tireless, energetic

and determined, with a mind of her own, who will seldom fulfil a man's dreams. It has been a woman's role to maintain the social order and traditions, and this obligation leaves little room for what are thought of as feminine traits, involving eroticism or the emotions. Although the women depicted in art have become more urbanized since the mid-twentieth century, the role model of the rural wife forced by circumstance to adopt a position of strength has proved to be deep-seated. Now it is female artists and writers who have taken it upon themselves much more seriously than their male counterparts to portray urban life, the new attitudes towards conjugal relations, the division of labour between the sexes, social networks and post-modern identity.

The painter Helene Schjerfbeck is regarded as one of the most eminent Finnish women of all time and her paintings have for years been among the most valuable Finnish works on the international art market. Her reserved, timeless style is something that appeals to people regardless of nationality. Schjerfbeck's *Pukukuva I* (Dress I) is from 1908.

The gastronomic image of Finland grew as part of the creation of a national identity, so that both typical and exotic ingredients were sought in the forests, in the sea or in remote Lapland, such produce as bear and reindeer meat, salmon and cloudberries.

HOSPITALITY AND FINNISH FOOD AND DRINK

Finns often start their summer holidays near the end of June. They say summer's at its best then. People like to eat outdoors, like this family in the garden of their summer cottage.

Emphasis was also placed on traditional provincial specialities. Finland has several noteworthy culinary strengths, namely a long tradition of self-sufficiency which means that people have been used to preparing food from ingredients found close at hand and the strong, basically western, tradition in matters of food combined with many interesting eastern features. These Swedish/Scandinavian and Russian/European influences can be seen in both everyday meals and celebration dishes.

The food, cookery, eating habits and table manners of the Finns have altered greatly in the course of the last hundred years. In earlier times there were substantial differences in the type of food eaten by the various classes in society. In the days when only the well-to-do had sufficient food to eat, shortages and economising were part of everyday life for the underprivileged both rural and urban. Common to all, however, was pursuit of self-sufficiency and the storing of foodstuffs. The staple foods of the Finns were largely cereal-based, especially bread and porridge, which were supplemented with potatoes, root vegetables, peas and beans, salted or smoked meat, and fish whenever any could be caught. Rarer, more seasonal additions were garden produce and the wild berries and mushrooms that could be gathered in the forests. One distinctive legacy of those days is the continued popularity of nutritious dark rye bread above all other varieties.

Food has always linked the Finns with their country roots. The dairy farming practised alongside the growing of grain crops provided the people with butter, milk, cream and the soured milk known as *piimä*, so much so that milk products replaced water and home-brewed beer as the main beverages drunk with meals. One of the outstanding differences between western and eastern traditions lay in the design of the oven, which meant that in eastern parts of the country food was mostly stewed gently in a large oven, whilst in the west is was boiled over an open fire. People in the east favoured spicy tastes, while western Finns favoured sweet dishes, and whilst farms in the west produced soft cheeses, those in the east used mainly soured milk in the form of quark. Similarly, western Finland was the place for hard, sour bread and mellow foods, whereas people in the east would regularly bake soft loaves of bread and pies, including Karelian pies and various fish pies. Where a joint of meat would be roasted whole in the west, in the east pork and beef would be cut into cubes and stewed together in the oven to become what is known as Karelian stew. The movement of population to the towns during the twentieth century mixed these cooking traditions and brought about big changes in people's eating habits. Sour lost ground to sweet and since the Second World War each decade has brought

The delicacies on the dining table vary with the seasons. One of them is a selection of fish roes – as an hors d'oeuvres at Christmas or spread on *blin* pancakes in the early spring.

new products onto the market and new meals onto the dining table. Consumption of meat has increased, as has the popularity of ready-made foods. At the same time regional differences in what people eat have evened out, so that people eat more or less the same food all over the country. And despite the changes, the staple foods, dairy products, potatoes and bread, have retained their prominence. As living standards have risen, new problems have emerged. Illnesses caused by malnutrition have given way to ailments related to over-eating. On the other hand, functional foods, products that have a health-promoting effect, such as rye or products that reduce cholesterol, have proved to be popular offspring of Finnish product development, evidently linked to the fact that Finland has a long tradition of nutritional advisory services.

Alongside the changes in food, eating patterns have also changed over time. Where people were accustomed to eating a healthy, mostly savoury breakfast, followed by lunch and an evening meal, urbanization and the fragmentation of family life combined with the provision of midday meals in schools and workplaces have reduced the amount of food cooked at home and the number of meals that a family will eat together. The family meal is now largely something that takes place at weekends.

The Finns are hospitable people and it is still customary to fill the table with the best in the house when guests are invited. The Scandinavian buffet or 'smörgåsbord' tradition is part of the Finnish way of life and such meals invariably offer a splendid array of food. There are other traditional forms of hospitality, coffee drinking being one of leaders. Finland has the highest per capita consumption of coffee in the world and it is drunk everywhere, often accompanied by several kinds of bun, Danish pastries, doughnuts and biscuits. The aroma of freshly made coffee and the pastries that go with it form one of the many fragrances of this country.

Bilberries freshly picked from the forest and served with sugar and milk are a classic summer treat – as a dessert or for breakfast.

The cycle of the seasons is important in this respect, too. People are active in the summer, but the pace slows down in winter, and the seasonal transitions are often marked by particular festivals of their own: Christmas, Easter, May Day, Midsummer and All Saints' Day. Family events are also important. Baptisms, confirmations and school-leaving parties often take place at home, and thus become occasions for relatives to get together. Birthdays that represent "round figures", as the Finnish saying goes, usually from the 50th upwards, are similarly regarded as major causes for celebration.

There are many speciality foods associated with certain seasons or months of the year. January is a time for burbot, Russian-style *blin* pancakes and fish roe, and in February the accent is

on pea soup, the cream buns eaten on Shrove Tuesday and the cakes named in honour of the national poet, J. L. Runeberg. Easter brings a number of special delicacies enjoyed in March or April, the malted grain mixture known as *mämmi*, chocolate eggs, of course, and the traditional Orthodox Easter foods, *pascha, kulitsa* and *baba*. The typical foods for May Day are herring and *tippaleipä*, cakes made of a deep-fried, extruded doughnut mixture, washed down with a mead-like drink known as *sima*. The summer is the time to enjoy fresh fruit and vegetables, such as strawberries, currants, rhubarb and freshly dug new potatoes, and

Particular favourites of the national poet, J. L. Runeberg, were the little cakes baked by his wife, Fredrika. These are usually eaten nowadays around the time of his birthday, 5th February. The Finns appreciate a "good cup of coffee", which traditionally includes a pleasant chat and a plentiful selection of buns and cakes.

wild berries from the forests, especially bilberries, raspberries, lingonberries and cloudberries. In August the hunting season begins, and there are also crayfish to be had, and wild mushrooms, and by September the new season's grain is available for baking bread and apples can be harvested. In October the Finns look towards the sea, and many towns and villages hold a Baltic herring market. All Saints' Day, in November, marked the end of the farming year in bygone days. Now the month is treated as the beginning of the season of workplace Christmas parties, with festive food and mulled wine. Christmas is traditionally a time that the Finns spend at home, with plenty to eat, and tranquillity descends over the whole country for a few days.

EATING AND DRINKING OUT

Attitudes towards the licensed premises as an institution are a highly complex matter. In the agrarian society people ate all their meals at home and the inn was a legacy from the days of horse-drawn transport. The tradition of local inns licensed to sell beer and spirits nevertheless continued until well into the twentieth century. Meanwhile restaurants began to appear in the towns and near railway stations in the nineteenth century, and many towns still have a Town Hotel or Society House to remind people of those days. After the First World War, restaurants began to evolve in a manner distinct from those of Europe in general, chiefly on account of the Prohibition Law of 1919–1932 and the subsequent government policy of restricting the availability of alcoholic drinks and protecting the populace from the worst effects of drinking by controlling the sale and consumption of alcohol.

The Prohibition Law nevertheless had an effect on drinking habits that finally set the seal on the concept of the Finns having a "poor head" for spirits as part of the national self-image. Compliance with the law was strictly supervised, but double standards existed and smuggling was rife. The new law on alcoholic beverages introduced in 1932 did little to alter this mind-set as it was still close to prohibition. Drinking was viewed as a social problem and a matter of law and order, and this attitude of strict control and "teaching the people correct drinking habits" persisted in Finnish licensed premises right up to the 1960s. In fact the main elements of the supervision and licensing system are still in force today. Significant steps forward were taken in 1969, with the "freeing" of medium-strength beer for sale in food shops, and in 2004, with a sharp reduction in the tax on alcoholic beverages, but both resulted in a clear increase in the consumption of alcohol. Finland is still a country of

The elves, Santa's little helpers, are on the move everywhere just before Christmas, checking on whether children have been behaving themselves and have deserved their presents. All the smallest members of the family, at least, will wear a red elf's cap on Christmas Eve. Candles on the table or window ledges create a homely atmosphere all through the winter.

beer and spirits, although wine has increased in popularity among the urban middle-class. The tradition of home-brewed beer has survived most vigorously in the lake region of central-eastern Finland, where licences have now been issued for the commercial brewing of the local *sahti*.

The Prohibition Law and its consequences left certain permanent marks on the character of Finnish restaurants. The European concept of the inexpensive, family-owned *café, pub*

Choir singing is popular. On May Day the YL Male Voice Choir traditionally sings spring songs and drinking songs on the hill of Ullanlinna in Helsinki, inviting the people gathered there enjoying champagne or sparkling mead to join in a true carnival atmosphere.

Anna-Maija Tanttu

Northern Flavours

otava

Traditional national foods have come back into favour in recent times, and local ingredients and old, original recipes are being enthusiastically adapted for the purposes of *haute cuisine.*

or *Kneipe* where one can drop in for a convivial drink is missing, having fallen foul of the strict drinking law for so long. The middle-class pub-style music bars of recent times are imports from Britain, Ireland and America, even to their fittings and décor, and the suburban and rural bars and neighbourhood restaurants selling medium-strength beer are frowned upon by the many people who find them not quite respectable enough. Even though alcohol policy has become more liberal, there is still a strong moralistic attitude attached to the subject. Finnish drinking habits have not become "Europeanized", not even in recent times, and "binge drinking" has remained a national characteristic that is handed down from father to son, and nowadays also from mother to daughter. The change in attitudes may be perceived in the fact that alcoholic drinks have taken the place of coffee as the centrepiece of official functions.

Finnish restaurants have altered in many ways in recent decades. With increasing immigration, ethnic restaurants have appeared, and trendy restaurants run by young gourmet chefs have increased vastly in numbers, especially in big towns, so that eating out has become far more a part of the Finnish way of life than it used to be, especially for the under-40s. At the same time, the coffee shop culture has undergone a renaissance and the Finns, who have traditionally been a nation of coffee drinkers, have now adopted many of the European varieties of coffee.

Food is now a hobby and topic of interest for many people, as reflected in the popularity ratings of TV cooks, the abundance of cookbooks on the market and the numbers of people enrolling for

food and wine courses. The attitude to food, at least, has become more European. Although the nature of the work has altered, families have become smaller and the old sense of community has faded somewhat, the need to experience high moments in the life has remained. The Finns still believe in celebrating not only family events, especially anniversaries and birthdays, but also graduations and achievements of all kinds, retirement, sports victories and other moments of success. New generations of Finns are taking up the old theme: put plenty of food on the table, invite your friends and enjoy an evening together.

Laura Kolbe, Ph.D., is Professor at the Department of History, University of Helsinki. She is a well-known historian and public figure in Finland.

The range of eating places is wide, from Michelin-starred restaurants to suburban kebab take-aways. The Savoy Restaurant, which specializes in traditional cuisine, is famous for its décor and the unforgettable scenery. The furnishings and tableware were designed by Alvar Aalto in 1937, and it is this restaurant in the heart of Helsinki that gave its name to his famous Savoy vase.

The Economy

The "green gold" of the forest industries formed the first pillar of the nation's industry. High-tech industries are crucial now. The Nokia phenomenon arose out of cable manufacturing and an industrial tradition. Formerly an agrarian country of modest stature, Finland now shares in European affluence and the global economy thanks to steady economic progress. The agricultural sector is undergoing far-reaching change.

Artists are no longer content with painting natural landscapes but are turning to textile printing that reflects urban life. Maija Louekari, *Moments*, 2003 (Marimekko).

Finland has experienced many economic miracles in its time that have raised it from the status of a remote underdeveloped country to that of one of the most affluent societies in the world. The last such event was the rise of Nokia to the position of the world's leading manufacturer of mobile phones. It was in effect Nokia that lifted Finland out of the recession in the early 1990s and set the economy on an upward trend once more.

Now people are asking where we are likely to find a new Nokia. The great hopes pinned on biotechnology have not borne fruit, at least not yet, and there is probably no real reason to expect the global economy to work wonders. Instead, it seems that the Finns will have to look for a number of narrow niches in which they can be successful. The world's great innovations have often arisen in restricted fields – from the Athens of ancient times to the garages of Silicon Valley in modern California. Why shouldn't it happen in this tiny country of Finland?

One thing is clear, however, that constant renewal will be needed. Plenty of this has taken place in the Finnish economy over

Industrialization began in the eighteenth century with rural ironworks and sawmills. An ironworks would usually gather a small cluster of buildings around it in the midst of vast expanses of fields and forests.

recent years, but its structures are in many cases far too rigid, as is true elsewhere on the "old" continent of Europe. The Finns have nevertheless shown that when the crunch comes they are capable of taking huge strides forward and developing a spirit of national unanimity in economic matters as in other walks of life.

The first economic miracle that Finland achieved was its take-off on the path of industrialization with the rise of the wood processing industry in the 1870s. It is true that exports had relied on the bounty of the forests since the Middle Ages – first furs, then tar derived from wood and finally sawn timber from water-powered mills, but this had not been enough to prevent Finland from suffering the last major peacetime famine to occur in western Europe, in the 1860s, with the loss of 100 000 lives, or 5% of the population.

It was above all timber exports to Britain that freed the country from the vicious circle of poverty, the decisive factor being the development of steam-powered sawmills and new transport possibilities – largely thanks to entrepreneurs from Norway and Sweden. The new Nokia Company began the production of mechanical wood pulp in 1866, and this was soon supplemented with chemical pulp and paper, much of which was exported to Russia.

The gross national product per capita doubled over the period from the 1860s to the First World War, and incomes from tree harvesting and the sale of timber gradually spread into the

Lumberjacks were an important group of skilled workers in the golden age of sawmills. Harvesting the timber and transporting it in huge log rafts through lakes and rivers was an arduous and dangerous job. These bold adventurers became the heroes of numerous books, popular songs and films.

countryside, enabling people to buy cloth, ploughs, threshing machines and other goods which Finnish industry began to manufacture. This economic development was supported by exports of butter and other foodstuffs to Britain and to the nearby metropolis of St. Petersburg. The distribution of incomes remained uneven for a long time, but Finland did not fall into the same situation as Latin America, where export incomes either drained away overseas or were squandered on luxurious living by the established wealthy class and the nouveau riche.

The second economic miracle came after independence in 1917, when the loss of Russian markets was quickly compensated for by pulp and paper exports to the west. A huge copper mine was opened at Outokumpu, in eastern Finland, with government capital, and the economically crucial step was taken with the later development of the flash smelting technique. Export revenues together with the imposition of protective customs duties enabled the expansion of a wide range of industries serving the domestic market, and the Finnish economy was one of the few that thrived in the 1920s and 1930s in spite of the serious problems of the Depression. Thus, even under those conditions, Finland was able to keep up its reputation as "a country that paid its debts" to the United States and others.

The third miracle was economic recovery after the Second World War, despite the heavy burden of reconstruction, the problem of re-housing 400 000 displaced Finns from the ceded territories and the harsh reparation payments imposed by the victors, notably the Soviet Union, which were paid on time to the last dollar. In fact the manufacturing of military material during the war and industrial products as part of the reparations programme did much to stimulate the expansion of mechanical engineering and shipbuilding. Companies operating in these sectors gradually emerged as world leaders in the building of paper machines, icebreakers and luxury cruise ships. The Kone company, for its part, developed into one of the world's largest manufacturers of lifts and cranes.

These three economic miracles enabled the national economy to grow steadily up to the 1980s. A further miracle may be perceived in the fact that Finland was able to associate itself with western economic integration in spite of the suspicions expressed by its eastern neighbour, the Soviet Union. Finland belonged to GATT (nowadays the WTO) from the outset, and also to EFTA, and signed a free trade agreement with the EEC (nowadays the EU) along with the other EFTA countries in 1973. Thus it was a part of the western market economy all through the Cold War period, so that the Soviet Union did not normally account for more than 20% of its foreign trade. On the other hand, the economic system within the country continued for a long time along traditional lines. The banks were all-important, and were well aware of the power that they wielded, Finnish ownership was closely guarded and cartels were common.

The expanding economy allowed the Nordic welfare state system to be extended constantly. Employers and trade unions would conclude collective bargaining agreements that covered the whole country, applying to many social benefits as well as actual wages and salaries, and the government would support these agreements by promising tax and social welfare incentives.

The working week was reduced to below 40 hours, holiday rights were extended to five weeks per year in many cases, and provisions for child allowances, paid maternity and paternity leave, practically free health services, a comprehensive system of inexpensive day care places for children under school age, national pensions for all citizens of retirement age, partly income-related unemployment benefits and free education up to university level were added to the system in the course of time. This previously underdeveloped country had now risen to the position of one of the most affluent societies in the world. It also had one of the most even distributions of income – and one of the highest rates of taxation. "To be born a Finn is like winning a lottery," people would say.

WELFARE AND A LIBERAL ECONOMY

Here are some examples of the services provided within the Finnish welfare state. The details are sometimes rather complicated, so that these figures must be regarded as giving a general picture of the situation.

Salaries. The mean salary for regular employment is EUR 2,555 a month. A shop assistant, for instance, will earn EUR 1,933 on average, a bus driver EUR 2,223, a schoolteacher EUR 2,600, a manager in industry EUR 4,644 and a doctor EUR 5,030. Salaries for top executives are many times greater. Mean net incomes in industry after tax are approximately the same as in France.

The **working week** is normally 37.5 hours. Considerable bonuses are paid for Sundays, night work and overtime. **Paid holidays** usually amount to one month in summer and one week in winter.

The Social Insurance Institution is subordinate to Parliament and is responsible for ensuring the basic subsistence of the population, promoting health and assisting individual citizens to cope independently with all life situations.

Visits to **maternity and post-natal clinics,** including examinations by a doctor, are free of charge, and mothers and their children below school age normally make full use of these services. **Childbirth** in a hospital costs less than EUR 100. **Maternal or parental leave from work** with an allowance of about 70% of normal salary (minimum EUR 15.20 per day) is granted for just under one year, in addition to which the father is entitled to 18 working days of **paternity leave**. The mother or father then has the option of taking **child-minding leave** without salary on an allowance of at least EUR 294 a month until the child reaches the age of three years.

Child allowances of EUR 100–172 a month are paid for each child up to the age of 17 years, with no limit on parental incomes. **Child care** at a day nursery (cost EUR 0–200 per month) or with a family is arranged by the local authorities.

Education. Compulsory schooling (for 9 years) and tuition at upper secondary schools (for 3 years), vocational schools and universities are free of charge, as are textbooks and a daily meal during the period of compulsory education. Every university student receives a **study grant** of EUR 260 a month and an

accommodation grant of EUR 200 a month. Students at other institutions also receive study grants. In addition, the state acts as a guarantor for study loans.

Health. All Finnish citizens belong to the health insurance scheme. Hospitals and health centres are maintained by the local authorities. The maximum charge for a visit to a health centre doctor is EUR 11, and the daily maintenance charge at a hospital is EUR 26. The basic charge for a visit to a health centre dentist is EUR 7. The annual ceiling for public health service charges is EUR 590 per person. The health insurance scheme also refunds 60% of the normal fee charged by a doctor or dentist and at least 42% of the cost of medicines prescribed. A sickness benefit equivalent to 70% of salary (minimum EUR 15 per day) is paid for approximately one year.

Nordic walking, a form of exercise invented by the Finns, is a good way of improving one's fitness, being almost 50% more efficient than ordinary walking.

Income-related **unemployment benefits** (60% of previous salary on average, but as much as 90% for some low-paid categories) are paid for the first 500 days, after which a flat rate of about EUR 24 a day (with a supplementary child allowance) is paid on certain conditions.

The poor can receive discretionary support payments of at least EUR 373 a month, and an extensive system of **accommodation allowances** (averaging over EUR 200 a month) is available for those with very low incomes.

The official **retirement age** is between 63 and 68 years, but the mean age in practice is around 60 years. Pensions are normally the equivalent of about 60% of previous salary, averaging EUR 1,114 a month, with a minimum of EUR 525 a month for all citizens. Disability, unemployment and various other pensions are also paid, and war veterans receive supplementary pensions.

40% of the **costs of the social security system** are covered by salary-related payments made directly by employers, 11% by employees' social insurance contributions, 25% directly out of state tax revenues and 20% out of local taxes. The social security sector accounts for 26% of GDP.

INTERNATIONAL CONNECTIONS AND STRUCTURAL CHANGE Finnish companies went international in a big way in the 1980s, mostly through purchases of companies abroad. It was an expensive way to learn in many cases, but a nucleus of internationally successful businessmen gradually began to emerge. This was followed, however, in the early 1990s by a severe recession which transformed the whole economy and influenced the structure of society. At the worst stage unemployment was around 20%, production slumped and thousands of companies went bankrupt, mostly ones that had taken foreign currency loans, as the Finnish markka had to be devalued. The majority of the large group of savings banks disappeared, as did most of the labour-controlled cooperative movement. Nevertheless, the devaluation did succeed in restoring production by 1993, and around the same time agreement was reached on joining the European Union, an event that took place in 1995.

NOKIA LEADS THE RECOVERY The time was ripe for the fifth economic miracle. The Nokia Group, which had graduated from being a producer of paper, cables and rubber goods, became a manufacturer of computers and televisions by the 1980s, and decided then to concentrate on mobile telephony. A favourable environment for the breakthrough of GSM technology had been created, juridically and in other ways, and under the leadership of Jorma Ollila, Nokia sprinted into the lead in the furiously growing world mobile phone market of the 1990s, carrying a host of subcontractors, other partners and the entire Finnish economy with it.

Nokia design sells all over the world.

The country had already experienced the "casino economy" with its spate of company mergers in the late 1980s, but the real IT fever was to spread ten years later. Everything connected with it was supposed to turn to gold in an instant. The fever came to a sharp halt at the turn of the millennium, but Nokia had gained an established position as the world's leading manufacturer of mobile phones by that time and that branch of industry has continued to expand since. Nokia has also managed to maintain

Finland's economy has in recent years been bound up closely with the amazing success of Nokia. The company's rapid rise to the status of world's leading manufacturer of mobile phones was the driving force behind the economic recovery achieved in the late 1990s. The name Nokia still serves to strengthen the Finn's feeling of national identity, and the company continues to play an exceptionally prominent role in the economy of the country.

A small town in Finland and a telecoms giant

The homonym is no coincidence. It may come as a surprise to some that there is in central Finland a town named Nokia where the roots of the Nokia Corporation lie, more precisely on the banks of the Nokia River where a paper mill was built almost 140 years ago. The mill owner, surnamed Idestam, called his company Nokia, too, after the local manor, also called Nokia. The name Nokia is said to derive from the Finnish word, *nokinäätä,* a marten, an animal well-established in the Nokia region. The old Finnish word *nois* or *nokia* meant a black-furred sable.

"Nokia's success is built on its own industrial history and innovations,"says Björn Westerlund, the Nokia group's first CEO, who in his time was the key figure in laying the foundations of the modern Nokia. Some sixty years ago he dreamed, indeed believed, that electronics would have a great future. In 1956, he was appointed managing director of the Nokia cable factory and ten years later he took the helm of the Nokia Corporation, which then consisted of four manufacturing branches with companies producing cables, rubber, paper, and electronic equipment.

When Björn Westerlund realized, in the early 1960s, that the company's operations should be steered towards advanced technology, an electronics department was set up in the cable factory. It was also known as the "cancer ward", however, as it made a financial loss for the first 17 years of its existence. "I didn't mind that for years it cost more than it ever brought in. It was necessary to give those 'gyroscope geniuses' enough leash and space for experiments," Westerlund says.

Computers emerged as the flagship products of Nokia Electronics in the 1970s and in the next decade work began on the first generation of car phones using the NMT system. On the whole things did not go well for the company and by the early 1990s Nokia was in a state of crisis. It was then that Jorma Ollila, who had been invited to take up the position of CEO, decided to concentrate all the company's efforts on mobile phones, for which the GSM system had just been adopted.

The paper, rubber and cables divisions were sold off, as were the computers and many other interests. Nokia succeeded in devoting itself to the right field at just the right time and, with the support of a favourable national technology policy, emerged to lead the global market.

The best-known mobile phone manufacturer in the world is a company with a long, eventful history. Having previously produced paper, cables and rubber goods, it has had to redesign its trademark many times.

its profitability in the face of increasingly relentless competition and the partial standardization of mobile phone specifications. Apart from its efficient logistics and production systems, the company's continued success has also required enormous investments in product development, e.g. camera phones. Other firms which grew rapidly in partnership with Nokia were Elcoteq and Perlos.

The Nokia miracle, together with globalization, shook up the traditional structures of the nation's economy and its industrial sphere. Electronics overtook wood products as the country's main export sector, and although Nokia remained in a class of its own in this small country, other large concerns were strengthened through mergers or reorganizations. Most of the state-owned companies were privatized, as were numerous government agencies, and many international business practices were adopted, such as the granting of share options to top executives, with the attendant scandals.

When the restrictions on foreign ownership were lifted, Nokia and many other Finnish companies fell largely into external hands.

People all over the world are sailing in Finnish cruise liners and being carried in lifts built by Kone, including the latest models that are landscaped with Marimekko designs.

One of the biggest wood-processing companies, Enso-Gutzeit, merged with a Swedish partner to form Stora Enso, with a major part of the remaining forest-based industry grouping into UPM-Kymmene and M-Real. The dependence of industry on bank loans came to an end, and the stock market, which had previously been a relatively minor institution in Helsinki, gained in importance and became more international in scope. Hundreds of thousands of ordinary Finns set out eagerly to invest in shares – naturally with variable success.

All in all, heavy industry in Finland has become concentrated in just a few successful fields of operation. The manufacture of paper machines has become concentrated in Metso, which is also significant for its mining and quarrying technology, while the metallurgy sector is dominated by the formerly state-owned companies Outokumpu and Rautaruukki, and the chemicals company Kemira has a similar background. Huhtamäki is one of the world's leading manufacturers of packaging materials, Wärtsilä now specializes in large diesel engines, and the shipyards

THE CONCENTRATION OF PRIVATE ENTERPRISE

have been transferred to Norwegian ownership and have been particularly successful in the building of luxury cruise ships. The large state-owned electric power and oil companies were combined into a single Fortum group for a time, but the petroleum branch has now been segmented off again as Neste Oil.

The mighty commercial banks of old, KOP and the Union Bank of Finland, first merged together and were then fused with the Scandinavian bank Nordea, while the state-owned Post Office Bank was eventually

merged with the Sampo insurance company to form a "financial department store". This concern subsequently acquired the Nordic insurance group If, and some time later sold off its banking interests to Danske Bank. Meanwhile the Cooperative Bank group (OKO) has gone from strength to strength under Finnish ownership and has purchased Pohjola, one of the leading insurance companies. The other main forces in the insurance world are the mutual insurance company Tapiola and the major pensions assurance companies. Finland is unique in that its compulsory pensions scheme is managed by private companies.

In all these upheavals the cartels of earlier times have been broken up and former boundaries between company territories have disappeared. More competition has been introduced into retail trading, with the arrival of international firms such as Ikea and Lidl, but the cooperative S group and the K chain of private shopkeepers are still in a strong position. The furniture business is dominated by Isku, Korhonen, which makes the up-market Artek range of products, and a large number of smaller firms. The survivors in the clothing industry include Luhta, or L-Fashion, which concentrates on outdoor apparel, and Marimekko, while other design products are now concentrated in the Iittala Group. The farmers' cooperatives that have dominated the food industry for so long have been in a constant state of reorganization in recent times.

The national tree, the birch, lends its colours to the summer landscape throughout the country. It is favoured as firewood and its leafy twigs are the only proper material for making the whisks used in the sauna. It has also provided the bark needed for ancient handicrafts and the plywood used by Alvar Aalto in his curved furniture designs. The writer Zachris Topelius adopted it as a homely symbol in his tales and it has been a source of inspiration for the designers of furnishing fabrics, like Johanna Gullichsen.

As the "smoke-stack" industries become more concentrated and
assembly lines in particular are being transferred elsewhere, the
IT industry has been gaining in importance. This is reflected in
the numerous IT software companies, many of which have links
with Nokia. Partly as a consequence of the ill-fated UMTS auctions
in Europe, the former state-owned national telecommunications
operator was merged with its Swedish equivalent to form TeleSonera.
Telephone services have always been largely in the hands of private
companies in Finland, and these local operators have now combined
to form three major chains, Elisa, DNA and Finnet.

The large media concern SanomaWSOY has been transformed
from a family company into a public limited company quoted on the
stock exchange and has gone international and acquired interests
in more or less everything from the publishing of books and the
largest newspaper in the Nordic region, Helsingin Sanomat, to
the running of a television channel and a chain of cinemas.

The second major media concern, Alma Media, has recently
sold its MTV television channel to the Swedish company Bonniers
and is continuing as a large newspaper publisher, while the family-
owned publishing house Otava also controls the largest magazine
publishers in the country, Yhtyneet Kuvalehdet. Other regional
publishing firms such Gummerus, Kaleva, Turun Sanomat and
the "Central Finland" newspaper group are continuing in the
traditional manner, most of them as family businesses. The state-
owned Finnish Broadcasting Company (Yle) is financed through
television licence revenues, but like its counterparts elsewhere in
Europe it is currently going through a period of turbulence.

Other good representatives of the IT industry are to be found in
the form of the world's leading forest industry consultancy Jaakko
Pöyry and many other suppliers of specialized expertise.

Although there is a notable flora of small family businesses
flourishing alongside the large companies, industry in Finland
has always been dominated by the latter and many families have

FINLAND'S LARGEST COMPANIES IN 2006

Name	Sector	Turnover EUR million
1. Nokia	Electronics	41,100
2. Stora Enso	Forest industry	14,600
3. Neste Oil	Petroleum products	12,700
4. UPM-Kymmene	Forest industry	10,000
5. Metsäliitto (M-Real)	Forest industry	9,200
6. Kesko	Retail trading	8,700
7. Sampo	Finance and investments	7,100
8. SOK	Retail trading	6,800
9. Outokumpu	Metallurgy	6,100
10. Tamro	Medical wholesalers	5,500

PROMINENT FIGURES IN THE FINNISH ECONOMY

- Anne Brunila (1957–) is the first woman to be head of the organization representing the interests of the wood-processing industry. She was previously a government economist. forestindustries.fi

- Aatos Erkko (1932–), for many years Finland's leading newspaper publisher. Now retired from the media company Sanoma-WSOY, he still has a great deal of influence.

- Antti Herlin (1956–), CEO of the Kone Group, representing the fourth generation of owners of this family business famous for its cranes and escalators. kone.com

- Sirkka Hämäläinen (1939–) was the first woman to be Governor of the Bank of Finland and the first, and to date only, woman member of the board of the European Central Bank. She is now a board member of many large companies, including Kone and Investor, and the chairman of the board of the Finnish National Opera.

- Sixten Korkman (1948–), an economist appointed director general of the EU's Ecofin in 1995, he is now managing director of the Research Institute of the Finnish Economy and the think-tank Eva. etla.fi, eva.fi

- Olli-Pekka Kallasvuo (1953–), the CEO of Nokia, is Finland's top industrialist. He has a straightforward but efficient style. nokia.com

- Erkki Liikanen (1950–), a former Minister of Finance and long-serving EU commissioner, he is now Governor of the Bank of Finland, the country's central bank. bof.fi

- Mikael Lilius (1949–), chief executive of the energy giant Fortum, previously a successful businessman in Sweden. fortum.com

- Jorma Ollila (1950–), architect of Nokia's greatness, he is now chairman of the company's board of directors and that of the Royal Dutch Shell. nokia.com

- Mika Ihamuotila, a 43-year-old lion of the banking world, has exchanged his pin-striped suit for jeans and a velvet jacket by buying out Kirsti Paakkanen, 79, from the ownership of Marimekko. marimekko.fi

- Juha Rantanen (1952–), recently moved from the family company Ahlström to become chief executive of the precision steels manufacturer Outokumpu. outokumpu.com

- Björn Wahlroos (1952–), chief executive of the Sampo banking and insurance group. Once a youthful radical, then a professor, he is now a Friedman-style polemicist. sampo.com

lived for generations "in the shadow of the factory". Size and a plentiful supply of capital have always been necessary in the paper industry in particular, and family businesses have often suffered from the lack of a suitable successor. The Kone Company is still in the hands of the Herlin family, but the large, very traditional Ahlström Company is now in the process of quotation on the stock market, although the family that owns it has a couple of hundred members. The Ehrnrooth family, on the other hand, still hold a major stake in Fiskars and Wärtsilä.

The relatively small number of family businesses is a consequence of the fact that urbanization took place late in Finland and at world-record speed, so that the service occupations had little time to develop. Moreover, people who have only quite recently

Industrialization took place late in Finland, and it would be only a small exaggeration to say that up to the Second World War every Finn was able to milk a cow.

moved from the countryside to live in the towns regard it as a matter of honour that they are still able to make things with their own hands, but the concept of providing a service for others is often alien to them. And since the taxes on employing outside labour are high, the result is that this is to a great extent a "self-service" country. It is also the case, of course, that the most traditional of all branches of industry, wood processing, has always called for large amounts of capital, which family entrepreneurs in their time were seldom able to raise.

The previous staple occupations of the Finns, agriculture and forestry, have altered vastly in recent times. The crisis caused by the growth in the landless population at the beginning of the twentieth

FLUCTUATIONS IN AGRICULTURE

The forest is always close at hand. As much as 70% of the country's surface area is forest and an intimacy with nature is reflected in the character and lifestyle of the people and in the colours and forms that predominate in Finnish design. The domestic clothing and textiles industry has to respond not only to the demands of the northerly climate but also to the yearning for nature and nostalgie for the agrarian life felt by the urbanized population.

century not only contributed to the outbreak of the Civil War in 1918 but also led to a land reform by which a hundred thousand independent farms were created. More or less the same number were later established to house demobilised men returning from front-line combat and the displaced Finns moving from Karelia after the Second World War. The result was that by the early 1950s the country had a total of some 300 000 farms, mostly small ones. In most cases the main source of income during the winter months was forestry work, so that hundreds of thousands of men with axe and saw in hand set off into the snowy forests with their horses while the womenfolk remained on the farms to look after the small herds of dairy cattle.

By the 1960s the situation had changed. Hundreds of thousands of smallholders were moving into the towns or to Sweden, leaving their recently built houses to be used as summer holiday homes. The movement from the land was slowed down somewhat by the payment of agricultural subsidies and regional allowances. A much heavier blow to farming came when Finland joined the European Union in 1995, although the government did retain the right to make national agricultural support payments on a more or less permanent basis, as the country's ability to produce its own food continued to be accepted as a security issue as well as an occupational one.

In spite of the subsidies, the survival of farming in the

northernmost grain-growing country in the world in the face of European, not to mention global, competition will call for an increase in farm sizes at least. Even in Germany a hectare of arable land produces twice as much grain as in Finland, where it is touch and go as every harvest time approaches whether the grain will ripen before the first night frosts set in, and where cattle have to be kept indoors for half the year.

Thus farm sizes have increased during the EU era and the number of farms has decreased rapidly. Even so, it has been difficult for the Finns, with their conscientious Protestant upbringing, to adapt to the bureaucracy of EU agricultural policy, which is perhaps looked on in a more relaxed manner further south. The Finns value their locally produced food, which contains smaller amounts of industrial chemicals than imported produce, and efforts have now been made to specialize in health-promoting, functional foodstuffs and such unusual but interesting specialities as reindeer meat.

Greater efficiency has also been introduced into forestry, so that horse-drawn sleighs and lumberjacks wading through snow have been replaced by advanced mechanical harvesters. In fact the country's timber reserves are evidently greater now than at any time since records began. Felling is governed by strict regulations, and reforestation is expected to begin at once. Vast bog areas are being mined for fuel peat, and when the reserves at a site are exhausted the area is planted with trees, turned over to farming or allowed to revert to a natural state. There are also extensive national parks, primarily in the north.

Economic life has been through such an upheaval over the last couple of decades that even someone who is accustomed to following developments finds it difficult to keep abreast of all the mergers and changes in company names and ownership. All in all, Finland is nevertheless an affluent industrial country with a GDP that has been consistently growing faster than the EU average. Its

GLOBALISATION AND ITS CHALLENGES

KEY STATISTICS ON THE FINNISH ECONOMY

THE ECONOMY

	EUR
• GDP	168,000 mill.
of which taxes	43.5%
• gross income per capita	30,000
• net foreign debt	24,000 mill.
• state budget	41,000 mill.
• public EMU debt	66,000 mill.
• annual rate of inflation	1.6%

LABOUR FORCE

• services	69%
• manufacturing and construction	26%
• agriculture	5%

Total employed 2.4 mill.,
unemployed 204,000 (7.7%)

AGRICULTURE

• Number of farms	69,071
• mean arable area	33 hectares
• mean yield (wheat)	3.5 tonnes
• self-sufficiency (grain)	92–115% of consumption
• head of cattle	almost 1 mill.

FORESTRY

- forest 26.3 mill. hectares
- ownership: private 52%, state 35%, companies 8%, others 5%
- tree species (by volume): pine 50%, spruce 30%, deciduous 20%
- annual increment in growing stock: 97 mill. m³
- commercial felling per year approx.: 51 mill. m³

HOUSING

• total dwellings	2.7 million
• mean floor area	78 m²
• floor area per person	38 m²
• owner-occupied	58 %

MAIN BRANCHES OF INDUSTRY

	Employees	Value added EUR / billion / %	
Electronics/IT	60,927	7,187	21.⬛
Machinery, metal products	100,959	6,004	18.⬛
Chemicals	35,958	3,615	10.9
Paper	31,379	3,073	9.2
Energy	15,511	2,930	8.8
Foodstuffs	36,256	2,127	6.4
Printed matter	27,587	1,694	5.⬛
Metallurgy	16,289	1,630	4.9
Sawn timber, wooden boards	26,511	1,284	3.⬛
Vehicles	19,388	1,030	3.⬛
Ceramics, cement	15,160	1,163	3.⬛
Clothing, textiles	11,127	512	1.⬛
Furniture	9,906	451	1.⬛
Mining	4,348	348	1.⬛
Others	3,700	234	0.⬛
Total	415,016	33,279	100

TRANSPORT AND COMMUNICATIONS

• private cars	2.5 mill.
• road network	78,189 km
of which motorways	693 km
• railways	5,905 km
• merchant ships	642 / 1.6 mill. grt
• air passengers per year	16.3 mill.
• wired phones	2.1 mill.
• mobile phones	5.4 mill.
• Internet connections	1.5 mill.

SOURCES OF ENERGY

• oil	24%
• wood–based fuels	20%
• nuclear power	16%
• coal	15%
• natural gas	11%
• peat	6%
• water and wind power	3%
• electricity imports and others	3%

Total energy consumption 1479 PJ.

public sector economy is in good shape and the country managed easily to meet the EMU entry criteria. Unemployment has more than halved from its peak figures of some years ago, although there are still many people who can find work only through government job creation schemes

Many questions are being asked, however, about the future of Finland's relatively small-scale economy in the age of globalization and the transfer of production to China. What will there be left for Finland to produce? At the same time, the baby-boom generation will shortly be retiring and expecting to draw substantial pensions, but will we be able to find the necessary money? And how will we manage to maintain our other welfare services? Will we need a sixth economic miracle?

People are anxious to remind us that globalization, which is not, of course, a new phenomenon, has so far worked to Finland's benefit. Without participation in the international division of labour, the country would have remained a sparsely populated backwater which would never have been able to gain its independence, and perhaps not even uphold a culture or even a language of its own. One essential for the survival of a small economy is involvement in the global economy.

In fact it is only in a limited number of cases, although admittedly well publicized ones, that Finnish jobs have actually been shifted to the Far East, whereas the many Finnish businesses that have been set up there have done much to increase affluence at home. Product development and the higher levels of management have usually remained in Finland. The same is true of the cases in which production has been moved to Estonia and other low-cost countries.

RELYING ON INFORMATION AND EDUCATION

Finland's position in the world economy has greatly improved since the days when raw material supplies, capital and the availability of labour were the main factors required for economic growth. Other than the forests, its natural resources have always been limited.

Hydroelectric power has never existed on the scale to be found in Sweden, in spite of possessing a couple of hundred thousand lakes, and there are very few mines left, although some promising new discoveries of ores have been made recently. Even capital was so scarce up to the 1980s that the state had to assist in financing major manufacturing investments. Now the government has been able to sell most of its shares in such companies.

The principal success factor nowadays is intellectual capital – knowledge – the importance of which was indeed emphasized long ago in the national epic poem, the Kalevala. The Finns have always had a respect for schooling, and it has been a matter of honour for farmers and industrial workers to send their children to school, contrary to the situation in many countries with sharper class distinctions. The recent PISA survey published by the OECD rated Finnish teenagers the best in the world at reading and gave them very high marks in other subjects, although admittedly their skill at reading may be partly due to the fact that the Finnish language is phonetic, it is written as it is pronounced, and the fact that cinema and television films are subtitled in Finnish or Swedish rather than being dubbed.

A good basic standard of education is thus one of the advantages that Finland has. Similarly, its higher education system is extensive, although the standard is variable. On the other hand, the country has produced relatively few top scientists; the only Nobel Prize for science was that awarded for chemistry to A. I. Virtanen in 1945, appropriately enough for innovations connected with agriculture and financed by the dairying cooperative Valio. Greater emphasis has tended to be placed on the encouragement of talented individuals in scientific fields in recent years, however, and the universities have made an

FOREIGN TRADE

Main export commodities:

• metal products, machinery and electronics 60%
• forest products 21%
• others 19%

Main export regions:

European Union 57%, elsewhere in Europe 17%, Asia 14%, North America 7%, other areas 5%

Main trading partners:

Germany, Russia, Sweden, Britain, USA, China, Netherlands, France, Italy, Norway.

attempt to concentrate their efforts.

Another advantage that Finland has is its good transport and communications systems and other forms of physical infrastructure, and above all its "intellectual infrastructure". Surveys have suggested that there is less corruption than in any other country, contracts are honoured and payments are made as agreed. Finnish businesses have not needed to resort to lawyers at every turn. In a small country such as this everyone knows everyone else and it is relatively easy to get things done.

The Finns do of course also have their problems in the harsh competitive markets of this world. They are often very good technicians but clumsy as salesmen. A good invention will very often be abandoned in the course of converting it into a commercial product. Similarly, the dependable atmosphere within the country often leaves the Finns gullible and open to deception in the rough and tumble of the outside world.

RESERVED AND GULLIBLE

Their business culture is usually of a home-made but straightforward sort, partly influenced by the fact that most of the managerial staff are officers or NCOs in the army reserve and are accustomed to giving and receiving orders. A Finn will usually come straight to the point without disguising it in unnecessary pleasantries. Even in meetings people will tend to cut out the small-talk and go straight for a quick decision. This is a style that has caused difficulties even in joint Finnish-Swedish companies, let alone ones involving partners from further afield.

There are very few obvious branches of the economy on which Finland can rely in the future. Agriculture has declined in importance and only a fraction of the labour force of earlier times is required for harvesting timber from the forests. Production of paper, plywood and sawn timber, virtually all of which are exported, is ample to utilize the country's own forest reserves. In addition, a large amount of roundwood has been imported, mainly from Russia, although

WILL THERE BE A NEW NOKIA?

this latter country is now better placed than earlier to process its own timber resources. Waste paper is collected up fairly efficiently in Finland for recycling. No new pulp or paper mills have been built here for some time, as the aim nowadays is to build them close to the sales markets, but even so the forest-based industries are likely to remain important – together with the expertise required to run them and to build the machinery that they need.

The crucial issue in the electronics industry will be whether research and development and the manufacture of demanding new products can continue to be located in Finland, given that routine production has to a great extent been transferred to countries where costs are lower. The same will be true of mechanical engineering and other sectors. The Finns have traditionally been at their best when operating with demanding products, usually items of equipment "somewhat larger than a horse", such as icebreakers or paper machines, on a one-off basis or in small batches, although some smaller items have been extremely successful, such as the Vaisala meteorological sensors or the Oras high-tech water taps and other bathroom fittings.

Building and many other services will always remain in Finland, of course, even though they may be provided by chains that extend over national boundaries. The media are

Classics from different ages and different spheres of life: the Linux penguin, logo of the computer operating system developed by Linus Torvalds; the Suunto wrist computer, the dream of every fitness fan; and the orange-handled scissors made famous by Fiskars.

to some extent protected by the strange language spoken here, but their ownership, at least, is likely to become more international.

There have been dreams of "a new Nokia", the next economic miracle, possibly involving biotechnology, in which considerable amounts of both private and public money have been invested, but the results have not so far come up to expectations. The development work has often turned out well, but the process of commercialization and market access has been a slow and uncertain – not to mention the prospects of reaping any profits.

We should remember, however, that Nokia Electronics made a loss in every one of its first 17 years and that the global breakthrough in the mobile phone business took just as long. Are there any owners with that degree of foresight left in our age of the "quarterly economy"? It is fairly obvious in any case that for the next few years Finland will have to rely mainly on its present branches of production. It may be that in this post-industrial age we are no longer entitled to look for spectacular steps forward that will lift the nation's economy onto a new plane. The decisive step as far as industry is concerned is likely to be global networking – often in very narrow sectors. The accent will be on services.

When economic policy is viewed on a broad scale, one of the main considerations with regard to future success will be the kind of environment in which business and industry are expected to function. Finnish salaries are around the average for the industrialized countries, and although the IT boom spawned a group of millionaires thriving on options, well paid executives in companies are not so well paid as in most comparable countries and central and local government employees in Finland are distinctly poorly paid. Collective pay agreements in recent years have been moderate and there have been few strikes.

RESCUING THE WELFARE STATE

Salaries have nevertheless been determined on the basis of the average trend in productivity within the whole economy, which has been beneficial in the case of efficient branches in which automation

Forest industries are non-urban by nature, as both sawmills and pulp and paper mills grew up beside waterways, close to sources of timber. Some of the finest architects in the country were responsible for the industrial and residential buildings in forest industry communities. The Sunila complex designed by Alvar Aalto is an example of ambitious industrial architecture, a symbol of modern-day technological optimism that was immortalized by Hugo Backmansson in his painting of 1938.

can be extended but has placed a strain on those where little improvement in productivity has been possible. This is one reason for the sharp decline in the textile industry, for example, and for the slow development in the service sector. Further pressure in this direction has been exerted by the heavy taxation on labour, the main purpose of which has been to fund the high standards of social security. Employers are now calling for a shift to wage negotiations conducted at each place of work separately.

There has also been much discussion about whether support should be provided for "low-productivity work", e.g. in the service sector, perhaps even in the form of government subsidies. The trade unions have rejected this idea of creating a "cheap labour class" and have criticized the concept of the "working poor" that exists in the United States, while others believe that it is better for everyone to have work of some kind, and that "not everyone can be a Nokia product developer". There are even fears of unemployment being inherited from one generation to the next, forming a class of people existing almost entirely on welfare benefits. There has also been discussion of the obligation on unemployed persons to accept whatever work is offered.

One pertinent issue is that of taxation and the public sector economy. The majority of Finns accept high taxes as the price to be paid for high standards of social security and inexpensive public services, but many still ask whether the burden of social welfare may not be too great. Income tax is high even on moderate salaries, and it is reasonable to ask if this will drive young people to seek a higher standard of living abroad, as they are better prepared to adapt to the international arena than their parents were. All in all, taxation makes Finnish labour an expensive commodity.

The underlying principle in economic deliberation nowadays is the fact that Finland's future will have to be built on high standards of education and expertise and not on low wage levels, as other countries would always win in the latter situation. The problem, apart from that of reaching the top in a particular field, would seem to lie in the structure of higher education. Are we educating too many humanists and theorists and too few practical people with advanced professional skills – starting with plumbers and construction workers? Another major problem is the ageing of the population and the prospect of a shortage of labour in the future. Should immigration be encouraged? The answers to these questions will emerge from the political polemics of the years ahead.

Jyrki Vesikansa, Lic.Pol.Sc., journalist, is a well-known writer on economic history.

Design District is a new cluster of creativity in the heart of Helsinki where design-oriented artists and entrepreneurs in various fields can take advantage of real synergy.

Design has become an ever more comprehensive concept and its new status as an economic success factor and not merely an esoteric cultural phenomenon has been strengthened by the emergence of young designers and architects, as epitomized by the work of the design office Valvomo.

4

Education as Innovation

Education and the arts played a significant role in building both the nation state and the welfare state. A belief in education is important in a country where social development has been achieved through study and the acquisition of intellectual capital. There has been notable investment in schooling, basic research and "lifelong learning".

Helsinki University Library functions as the National Library, with legal deposit rights which mean that its Fennica Collection constitutes a complete record of everything published in Finland. This 'scholars' sanctuary' is housed in an Empire-style building designed by the architect C. L. Engel near the corner of the Senate Square, with other university buildings close by.

Finland has gained a world-wide reputation as a country which invests in education, science and research to an exceptional degree. Indeed, it has fared wonderfully well in international comparisons of the quality of education and learning in schools, national investments in research and development and levels of economic competitiveness. It is also known as a country which has gone for widespread adoption of information technology at a rare speed.

It is obvious that the success of the flagship of our electronics industry, Nokia, has occupied a key position in the development of the Finnish information society, not only improving its position among the world's leading manufacturers of mobile phones but also emerging as Business Week magazine's fifth most valuable global brand name in 2007, immediately in the wake of the American industrial giants. Nokia's success has done much to create an image of Finland as a pioneer of advanced technological expertise.

We are indeed faced with a fascinating set of contrasts. On the one hand, this is predominantly a country of forests located in the far north, with a sparse population living under relatively harsh conditions, while on the other hand, this population is exceptionally

The head offices of most of the leading high-tech firms can be found in the nucleus of the country's hottest technological development, Keilaniemi, the Helsinki region's own Silicon Valley. The futuristic architecture with its glass and steel structures symbolizes openness, a forward-looking approach and an optimistic belief in the future. To the left are the international headquarters of the Nokia Corporation.

Ears of grain waving gently in the breeze, a field of barley stretching as far as the eye can see and a small barn nestling on the edge of a forest: these sights are just as typical of Finland nowadays as they were hundreds of years ago.

well educated, living in a welfare society which makes more use of mobile phones and other forms of modern technology than most other countries in the world. One may very well ask where the stimulus for this exceptional progress came from and how Finland has managed to achieve its present position. Having been a largely agrarian society right up to the time of the Second World War, how did it succeed in transforming itself into a post-industrial society with a strong accent on education and research?

The Finnish aptitude for adopting new technology had in fact been noted long ago, for the Spanish journalist and diplomat Ángel

Around the beginning of the 20th century there were many organizations advocating equal, universal suffrage, which meant that women, too, should have the right to vote. This picture shows the constitutive meeting of the Finnish Working Women's Association in 1900.

Ganivet expressed surprise in his writings in the late nineteenth century at how practical and technical inventions had been taken into use "eagerly, quickly and thoroughly" in Finland. He wondered, for example, at how the telephone was just as much an everyday household appliance as kitchen utensils, so that anyone who wanted to hear someone else's opinion would simply pick up the phone and ask "as if the interlocutor was in the same room". People in Spain, he claimed, were in general still very suspicious of the telephone. He also pointed to the exceptional equality of status enjoyed by women and was particularly amazed by the fact that they went around on bicycles just as the men did! There was great enthusiasm for progress in Finland even in those days, and it showed in people's everyday lives.

From the late nineteenth century onwards Finland was overtaken by a process of social change that transformed it from an agrarian society into an industrial one, and it was education that lay at the heart of this development. Decisive improvements were achieved in the levels of education leading up to university studies, and this created suitable conditions for the rise of a strong middle class. Also, the early introduction of compulsory schooling ensured that whole generations of children were systematically provided with a basic education.

The outstanding feature of the Finnish educational system in recent decades has been the network of universities, which is particularly extensive relative to the country's small population. The development of this system was one aspect of the government's regional policy, and it resulted in a network of 20 universities distributed throughout the country, which must be a record number per head of population. The system has now been filled out with a new network of 29 polytechnics. This policy of decentralization has done much to stimulate regional development and even out the opportunities for acquiring a university education, a further manifestation of the Finnish principle of equality. One consequence, however, is that the individual universities are relatively small.

The text in Finnish is Francis Bacon's adage "Knowledge is power". The owl of Minerva, symbol of knowledge and wisdom, presides over textbooks in a publisher's advertising poster from the 1930s.

All in all, the Finns believe in the power of education and the public sector has for the moment been prepared to invest in it to a reasonable extent, as the figure of 6.1% of GDP in 2004 represents a good average level internationally. Government spending on higher education in particular is generous by international standards.

The immense interest shown in education is linked to the country's history. It was the strengthening of the role of the middle class in society from the early years of the twentieth century onwards that instilled in people's minds the notion that education (rather than family background) was the gateway to moving up in society and that it promoted social equality. Many measures were adopted to encourage people to obtain a good education, including the guaranteeing of free education for all citizens, and it is still the case that the institutional education system is financed almost

THE FINNISH EDUCATIONAL SYSTEM

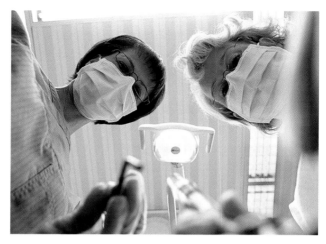

Dentistry and medicine as a whole are very much female-dominated professions, and other fields of tertiary education are steadily moving in the same direction.

entirely out of public funds. Even tuition at the universities is more or less free of charge. Private funding is in this sense of very minor significance by international standards.

Another unusual feature is the prominent position of women as recipients of education. Ever since 1987, they have been in the majority as far as awards of higher university degrees are concerned, and the pace has accelerated in more recent times so that the rise in the number of graduates is increasingly becoming attributable to the academic performance of women. The number of degrees obtained by women rose by almost 50% over the period 1991–2001. All disciplines have been affected except for medicine and dentistry, where the proportion of women graduates was already high at the beginning of that period.

A third feature of the "Finnish model of education" is the powerful adult education sector and the philosophy of "lifelong learning" that has been in vogue for many years and is reflected in a lively adult education and workers' education movement. Surveys have suggested that the Finns are among the most diligent seekers of education in the OECD countries at all levels, including adults. The current notion of "lifelong learning" has in fact caught on in Finland simply because it was already a part of everyday life. The Finns as a nation are exceptionally well disposed towards education.

The role of education in society can be viewed in two ways. It can be seen either as a service produced by society, the quantity and quality of which is determined by the financial and cultural resources available, or else as an active force within society and ultimately as a source of the knowledge and expertise required for developing the economy. In Finland, as in other countries that are endeavouring to become a knowledge-based society, it is evident that the latter interpretation is gaining ground. In an economy that is becoming increasingly reliant on knowledge creation, development of the educational sector has emerged as one of the key strategic issues. The theory goes that education will increase knowledge, which will improve the productivity of labour, and this in turn will generate new affluence. The education provided by society is thus regarded as a means of increasing the nation's intellectual capital, and Finland wishes to be at the forefront in achieving this.

The basis of the educational system lies in the 9 years of full-time, compulsory primary and secondary schooling arranged by the local authorities. Children start compulsory schooling relatively late by international standards, usually only at the age of seven. Prior to this they usually attend nursery schools, the majority of which are also run by the local authorities, including pre-

Finnish schoolchildren came out top in the Programme for International Student Assessment survey (PISA). The compulsory schooling phase, which is free of charge for all pupils, lasts nine years, beginning at the age of seven. Particular attention is paid to group work in schools.

Mm Maan al·la

am	sam	ma	mai	mar
em	rem	me	mei	mer
om	lom	mo	moi	mol
um	rum	mu	mui	mus

42

Careful attention is paid to the quality of textbooks by employing the best writers and illustrators available. All teaching materials, including books and items of equipment required for compulsory schooling, are financed out of public funds.

school classes in their final year. The aim of the public sector day care system is to enable young mothers to return to full-time work. The compulsory school system operates in a uniform manner throughout the country, thus offering every child the same learning opportunities and going as far as possible towards eliminating alienation and social differentiation. Here again there is a strong undercurrent of equality and an understanding of education as a resource for the whole of society, not just for the children themselves or their families.

There is not the same distinction between ordinary and elite schools in Finland as one finds in many other countries, and schools do not differ radically in the socio-economic background of their pupils. It is only in the bigger towns that perceptible social distinctions occur between residential areas and home backgrounds. Well over half of each age group complete the upper secondary school stage, which is intended for all pupils wishing to study at this level. There has been a major expansion in education for youth and young adults in recent years, and the general trend has been above all towards greater equality in this sphere.

There has been a certain decentralization of the Finnish school system since the late 1980s, and the upper secondary schools in particular have been encouraged to specialize in such subjects as music or mathematics. This trend may perhaps have introduced a new element of elitism, but it has at the same time created better opportunities for particularly talented individuals to develop their own strong points at this age. One outstanding feature of the Finnish school system is the emphasis placed on languages. Most pupils will study three or four languages in addition to their mother tongue.

As far as the international ratings of Finnish schools are concerned, it is worth noting that the OECD Programme for International Student Assessment (PISA) place Finnish teenagers in a very high position for reading, acquisition of information, comprehension and interpretation of written material, and for their knowledge of nature. They fared less well in discussion, evaluation and critical argumentation. In other words, the teaching of knowledge and skills is of a good standard, but we still have a long way to go in creative and reflective ability.

It would seem that the egalitarian ideal is realized fairly well in Finnish education, both regionally and between schools and also between the sexes, and the distinctions between social groups are among the smallest in the OECD countries. Pupils also receive free school meals as well as free tuition and study materials. The fact is that the school system has been fairly successful in combining quality with equality. Attempts have also been made to attribute the good results to the cultural and linguistic homogeneity of the population of schoolchildren. It is also significant that as many as 60% of entrants pass the Student Matriculation Examination, another high figure by international standards.

On the other hand, the Finnish school system still has problems to face. A comparative survey by the World Health Organisation (WHO) has shown that Finnish children enjoy being at school less than their peers in any other country in Europe. This illustrates the challenging fact that Finnish children and young people are unhappy at school but achieve good results there. It appears that in the future they will have more need for schools in which they can feel at ease.

Practical education in Finland is concentrated mostly in vocational schools. Apprenticeships based on direct attachment to a place of work is a less common practice than in many

other countries. The most significant structural reform in the whole Finnish educational system in recent times has been the introduction of the network of polytechnics, a form of practically oriented tertiary education tailored to the needs of business and industry that has been built up out of former vocational schools and colleges. Apart from being a part of the educational system provided for young people, these have also developed into a significant source of adult education.

Finnish undergraduates are somewhat older than their counterparts in many other countries on entering university, being mostly over 20 years of age at the time. The universities have experienced a phenomenal growth in student numbers in recent decades and in the number of degrees taken, masters' degrees having increased by 50% over the last 20 years and doctorates by virtually 100%. Over 40% of persons aged 25–34 years have a university degree or the equivalent, again an excellent figure by international standards. A controversial feature of Finnish tertiary education is, however, that the time taken to qualify for a degree is unusually long.

The persistent, fairly high level of unemployment in Finland has been predominantly a problem affecting the academically underprivileged and is partly a product of the exceptionally wide educational gap between the generations, the oldest age groups having a much lower average level of education than the extremely high level of the younger generations. Regardless of that disparity, rates of employment in Finland at all levels of education are exceptionally high compared with other EU countries. Apart from educational differences, there are other, structural, factors responsible for the high rate of unemployment. Even though the Finnish government set itself the ambitious target at the start of the new millennium that 70% of each age class should obtain a university or polytechnic qualification, there has been discussion recently as to whether this is a rational goal, especially in view of the fact that a considerable number of people nowadays who

Finnish schoolchildren today receive meals free of charge, but in the 1930s, and for some decades thereafter, children still brought sandwiches to school or paid a small sum for their school meal.

have such a qualification are not engaged in work commensurate with their educational standard. Spokesmen for industry have also maintained that higher education is overrated and that the greatest need in the future will be for skilled workers in a wide variety of trades.

The universities and polytechnics themselves have placed much emphasis recently on branches of study for which there is a great demand in industry, such as electronics and information technology, and have acknowledged that the most serious problem in these areas is the shortage of suitable students. In view of the burgeoning of the ICT cluster over the last ten years, it appears that Finland has had to harness the whole of its mathematical talent to meet the demand in that sector.

One of the main challenges for our educational system will be internationalization. The numbers of foreign researchers and students are still very low, so that only 2% of the students entering higher education in 2001 were foreigners, whereas the average for the OECD countries was almost three times higher. At the same time, Finnish students are more eager than ever to go abroad,

The highest academic award is the black, silk-covered doctor's top hat, which is worn by both men and women. Those who have successfully defended their doctoral thesis will be presented with this hat at a separate promotion ceremony arranged by each university every few years. Distinguished foreign persons can be awarded an honorary doctorate from a Finnish university.

either as exchange students while at school or to study at a foreign university. Looking to the future, and bearing in mind the ageing of Finland's population, the key question for the Finnish educational system will be whether we are able to attract sufficient numbers of talented foreign students to enrich the life of our educational establishments and workplaces.

Other challenges will be posed by globalization, the rapid changes taking place in the world, the accelerating pace of technological development and the passing of organizations of all kinds into the hands of experts and specialists. As far as students are concerned, these changes will create the need for improved ability to organize and analyse information, to learn new things all the time, to adopt a problem-centred approach, to employ creative thinking and to master broad cultural factors. Similarly it will be important for them to receive training in the communication skills required for successful teamwork and the knowledge necessary

Finns read a lot of newspapers. Most families subscribe to a morning paper, which they read over breakfast. There are numerous provincial newspapers which serve this purpose, competing for readership with the main national daily. Swedish-speaking Finns have their own newspapers.

for the efficient processing of information.

The concepts of knowledge and the nature of the learning process are themselves undergoing change at the present time. Even though the Finnish educational system discharges its basic duties excellently, it remains to be seen how well it will be able to adapt in the future to the challenges of a networked society and a knowledge-based economy. Teaching methods in schools are still highly traditional and place the accent on mechanical, teacher-centred learning. Also, the closure of some schools has meant larger classes in the remaining ones, giving rise to problems and preventing the guidance of pupils at a sufficiently personal level. In this respect significant new inspiration could be obtained from alternative pedagogical theories.

GROWTH IN RESEARCH AND DEVELOPMENT It is impossible to comprehend the role and significance of education in Finnish society without considering its close connections with research and development. International comparisons in the late 1970s were still showing Finland to be hopelessly lagging behind its competitors in R&D investment, which amounted to less than 1% of GDP. From that point onwards, however, first the public and then the private sector began to increase its investments and the gap was gradually closed. By the early 1990s Finland had reached the average level for the European Community of about 2% of GDP.

At that point the Finnish economy plunged into an unprecedented recession, whereupon the favourable trend in R&D investment came to an end, the GDP dropped and the public debt rose out of all proportion, so that public sector spending had to be severely cut back. It was just then, however, when the future was looking particularly bleak, that a new national strategy based on knowledge and expertise was drawn up with the aim of creating a knowledge-based society. At the core of this strategy was a resolve to invest significantly in raising levels of education and to increasing the R&D input to the level achieved by the top industrialized nations of the world. This was duly done and results followed. The country found its way out of the recession and rapidly established itself as one of the world's high-performance modern economies, being ranked ahead of the USA in the World Economic Forum survey of 2003 and attaining comparably high positions ever since. How did this come about?

One factor was the development from the early 1990s onwards of an innovation system based on strategic forecasting, in which the main public sector actors were the Academy of Finland, responsible for financing research, the Technology Development Agency TEKES, financing technology and development projects, and the National Fund for Research and Development (Sitra), concentrating on improving the country's competitive potential and promoting innovations. Above all, the contribution of Nokia was decisive in this, as the company alone was responsible for 25% of the nation's R&D investments. In the wake of Nokia's success, Finland developed a powerful, export-oriented ICT cluster in the 1990s that nowadays accounts for a third of the country's exports. This rapid expansion was attributable very largely to the

R & D investment in selected countries (% of GPD)

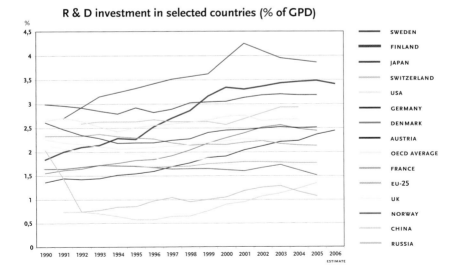

oi hora oriencia tuam q̃itus excedis / Et q̃nisq̃ fui
stin ges ad me si cibus. Nan aires mundi honores, nec eui
anuetos, gaus cu me habueris, oia dulcescut tibi. Et cu
tu me p̃ter dilexis, oia p̃er in que mundi sut amara
fient tibi quasi venenum...

Cp̃s dicit sponse q̃ ipe uult dictare ore suo propo istam
nouam regulam, quam uult ee monialiuz ad memoiaz
z honorem gloriose urginis maie matris sue. J.C.

Ane igitur religione ad honorem
amantissime mais mee. per muli
ores pmbꝰ z principaliter instituere
uolo. Cuius ordinem z statuta ore
meo proprio plenissime declarabo...

C In pncipio huiꝰ regule eps fun
dat eam sup tres utiutes. S. humili
tatis, castitatis z paupertatis. Probi
bens monialibus q̃ nichil habeant propriuz. Et abba
tissa prouideat eis de oibꝰ necessaryꝰ. S. y. C.

Pncipium itaq̃ huiꝰ religiois z salutis, est ua humi
litas. Et pura castitas. Atq̃ uoluntaria paupttas.
C Ideo nulli liceniꝰ sit habe aliq̃ propriuz, nullaz
oio rem, quaiꝰ minimam. Et nec obolum quidem
possidere, uel actiutate maibꝰ, nec auro qd habe til ange
h. nisi forte pro intextura alicuiꝰ opis, aliquil argeti tactu
opus sit. Et hoc z no absq̃ ꝯsilioꝰ licencia abbatisse.

C Oia aut necessaria ꝝ abbatissa speranda sut. S. indume
ta regulaia. lectisternia, z instrumenta opis, nec quidq̃
habeant quod regula no pmittit...

C Et pꝰ disponit hic quales lectos z lectisternia habeant
moniales. Tercium Capitulum

Sciendum e aut q̃ lectisternia regulaia ee debet
de straminibꝰ. sup illa uo fiant duo toralia de bu
rello sine linteaminibꝰ z culcitris. Sub capite

high standards reached in education and research.

With R&D expenditure equivalent to 3.4% of GDP in 2006, Finland can be said to have achieved an astounding rate of growth in this respect from the mid-1990s onwards, although this has now come to a halt. This has nevertheless placed it among the leading countries in the world table for R&D investment. Moreover, about 70% of this investment came from the private sector, a high figure by international standards.

Scientific research in Finland has also increased greatly in volume since the early 1990s and has become more international. Membership of the European Union from 1995 onwards has done much to stimulate European cooperation, and at the present time Finns have the fourth largest number of articles published in scientific journals in the OECD countries and about 2% of the working population are engaged in R&D, the highest proportion in the OECD. Finland is now regarded by many observers as one of the first countries to be moving towards a genuinely innovation-driven, knowledge-based economy. This entails, above all, a consistent policy of investment in education and R&D work, quality and effectiveness in the basic educational and research frameworks, and co-operation between the public and private sectors.

A chain of centres of excellence has now been set up by the Academy of Finland to support areas of study in which the country is among the world's elite – and there are a surprising number of such disciplines, ranging from neural networks to ancient civilizations (for more details, see www.aka.fi).

Modern Finnish technology and expertise can be applied equally well to the computer-aided stemmatological study of ancient manuscripts as to the developing of wrist computers.

FUTURE CHALLENGES Investment in education and research has become an integral part of the process of supporting the Finnish welfare state. It has proved possible so far to maintain the requisite infrastructure and its services fairly well in spite of persistent high unemployment, and the development of human capital has been recognised as an essential force behind social development and economic progress. The educational system is comprehensive, is fairly well resourced and has achieved much international recognition.

Whilst the main emphasis in R&D has so far been on technological innovation, the challenges of the future are likely to lie more in the field of social and cultural innovation. A good example of this is the Finnish system of paternal leave, enabling fathers to look after their small children for a time. Another could be the pioneering of new educational practices, e.g. the entrepreneurial training provided at the Team Academy attached to Jyväskylä Polytechnic, in which there are no lectures or examinations but the students learn by starting a firm of their own during their study time, or perhaps the music-oriented upper secondary school at Kaustinen, where the teachers function as coaches while the pupils take responsibility for certain important aspects of the school's activities, such as the circulating of information. There are thus plenty of opportunities for developing the educational system. It would also be important to create more means of systematically supporting talented individuals, although not in a way that would compromise our status as an egalitarian society. Particular challenges for Finnish education and research in the future will arise from the ageing of the population, the pressure on our universities to become more international and the development of collaborative networks. Methods will have to be developed to enable better utilisation of the progress achieved in certain areas of cultural and creative ability. One good example of this is the well-developed network of schools and colleges of music, by virtue of which Finland has produced a remarkable number of world-class musicians.

The key challenge and opportunity, for our educational system, and especially for universities, will lie in becoming more international. As the world opens up and European integration proceeds, our educational system will encounter a world that has not previously existed. The Bologna Process implemented by the European Union represents the most ambitious higher education reform in its history, the basic idea being that of a flexible, uniform European educational system capable of competing on the global education market. It will challenge Finnish tertiary education to become truly international and raise teaching standards to the highest international class, as has happened in the case of the compulsory school system, and in the research and ICT sector. Finland is well equipped for this challenge.

A major requirement in setting the goals for a renewal of the educational system will be the understanding that the needs of working life everywhere have altered fundamentally within a few decades, providing far more scope for creativity, problem-solving and a holistic approach. In order to develop these skills, people will have to be guided more purposefully towards discovering their own personal strengths that enable them to function in society. In other words the challenges for the future include how to introduce into the system more interaction, creativity and truly perceptive learning about human actions and motives. We Finns are already known for our diligence and sense of responsibility. Let us hope that we will be known in the future for our creativity, too.

Markku Wilenius, Ph.D., is professor of futures studies at the Turku School of Economics and Business Administration and director of the Finland Futures Research Centre. He is also Senior Vice-President of the German-based Allianz Group, one of world's leading financial services companies.

5

Politics and Society

A national awakening in the 19th century led to the building of
a Finnish state. The next stage was the welfare state. Regional,
social and sexual equality are powerful ideals. The role of local
and central government institutions is strong. The Finns trust
in their system and are law-abiding citizens.

The statue *Lex* by Walter Runeberg (1838–1920) depicts the lion of Finland, a sword, and the shield of the
Constitution protecting a maiden, later known as the Maid of Finland, with a bear hide as her headdress. This
motif is repeated in a number of other places in Helsinki, including the monument to Tsar Alexander II in the
Senate Square, the ceremonial stairway of the House of the Estates and the Presidential Palace.

A SCANDINAVIAN REPUBLIC

The basic intellectual structure underlying Finnish civil society is the Scandinavian notion of a free peasant community. There has never been a feudal system in Finland on the lines of that further south in Europe, let alone the Russian model.

A second deep-rooted principle has been that of representative government. Representatives of the people of Finland gained the right to take part in electing their ruler, the King of Sweden, more than six hundred years ago, and although the principle lay dormant for some centuries and altered in its manifestations in the course of time, the basic notion remained alive. Thus the constitution of the present independent state of Finland has a powerful undercurrent derived from the constitutional monarchy of Sweden that was preserved through the period of Russian rule. Taxation was based, at least in principle, on the compliance of the taxpayers, and the common people had the right of appeal directly to their ruler, over the heads of those in government. These seeds of democracy were refined and supplemented later by the precepts of parliamentarianism, the western judicial system and human rights.

The Finns are proud that their women became the first in Europe to be allowed to vote and stand for office in general elections. That was in 1906. From that time on equality between the sexes has been an important aspect of social and educational policy and a universally accepted principle in the country.

When Finland gained independence towards the end of the First World War it already had an administrative machinery that had grown up during the period of autonomous government under Russian rule and eventually even a parliament of its own. Thus the country's first constitution was built up upon these, and its central elements still serve as the basis for the present one. Apart from Great Britain, Finland is the only European country that was involved in the Second World War whose constitutional order has remained in principle unchanged from that time onwards into the third millennium.

The military battles with the Soviet Union during the war and the political struggles against Soviet domination during the Cold War period gave rise to a certain national consensus that operated in the background of the country's internal politics for decades in spite of fierce power struggles, and it was this consensus-based national self-assurance that created the foundation for establishing a welfare state on the Scandinavian model. Subsequently the dynamics and high standards of education achieved by this welfare state have created excellent conditions for generating a globally oriented information society.

The Finnish governments of the early independence period, and even those of the Cold War period, tended to be short-lived. No sooner had a new government assumed power than negotiations were started over the composition and programme of its successor. From the 1950s until the late 1970s the Soviet Union was able to exert pressure through its military consultation agreement and influence the composition of governments and at times even their actions. The improved economic conditions and social climate of the 1970s nevertheless allowed governments to remain in power for longer and it has been normal since the 1980s for them to last out their whole four-year term without difficulty.

In recent times each government has contained two of the three main parties, the Centre Party, successor to the Agrarian Party, the

POLITICAL STRUCTURES

Finland joined the European Union in 1995 and began using the euro in 2002. Finnish euro coins show images from nature, such as swans or the cloudberry, with the heraldic lion on the reverse side.

Social Democrats and the conservative National Coalition party, accompanied almost invariably by the Swedish People's Party, the broadest-based of all having been the coalition of 1995–2003, which contained all three of these main parties together with the Left-Wing Alliance, continuing the traditions of the communists, the Swedish People's Party and for part of the time the Greens as well.

During the Cold War the President was the person responsible for foreign and security policy, with the Foreign Minister a trusted aide, but the removal of the Soviet threat and membership of the European Union have allowed a normalization of security policy and a strengthening of the parliamentary responsibility of the Prime Minister in foreign affairs, as under the new constitution decisions concerning the EU rest solely in the hands of the government. This has substantially reduced the powers of the president relative to the first constitution adopted upon the gaining of independence, in which the regulations relating to the exercise of supreme power within the country had inherited certain monarchial features from the times of Swedish and Russian rule.

Most of the Finns who were in favour of joining the EU no doubt had the idea at the back of their minds that membership would improve national security, even though it does not as such provide any military guarantees. Thus, in spite of its official security policy of military non-alliance, Finland has been taking an active part in both EU and NATO-led military operations of a crisis management nature.

Finland decided to join the EU on the basis of a referendum in 1994, doing so at the same time as Sweden and Austria. In the early years of membership the popularity of the EU declined somewhat more slowly than in the other two countries, but nowadays there is a great deal more criticism of the EU than in most other member countries, so that it is only in Great Britain and Austria that the union's popularity is lower than in Finland.

The most serious problems of adaptation to the EU were experienced in agriculture, particularly since the regulations governing support for less favoured areas do not directly take account of the special features connected with a northerly location. The rectification of this discrepancy at the political and bureaucratic levels has entailed very strained negotiations at times, in which Finland has in the end been relatively successful.

The farmers have let their dissatisfaction be known, but not so vociferously as in some parts of continental Europe. Adaptation of the production of foodstuffs to the requirements dictated by the Common Agricultural Policy proved reasonably successful. The small farms that had become unprofitable were forced to abandon production, and the average size of the active farms increased. Correspondingly, the incomes of the surviving farming population rose faster in the late 1990s than those of other sectors of the population, who were just recovering from the effect of the recession. Agricultural incomes declined again in the early years of the new millennium, however, at the same time as those in industry and the service sector rose sharply in real terms.

Finland has 14 seats in the European Parliament and its nominated member of the new European Commission under José Manuel Barroso has special responsibility for the EU enlargement programme. The first EU Ombudsman was a Finn, as was the first chairman of the Military Committee, and when the European Central Bank was created in 1999 the Governor of the Bank of Finland was appointed to its board for the first 5-year term of office. The highest-level EU bureaucrats nowadays occupy leading positions in the departments of employment, social affairs, the environment and private enterprise.

PARLIAMENT

Finland has had a system of universal suffrage since 1906, when the right to vote was extended to women. General elections operate on a system of proportional representation that favours the larger political parties. 42% of the current members of parliament are women.

Parliament is responsible for choosing the Prime Minister

and for approving the government's policy programme, after which the government has a relatively free hand in practice, provided its actions remain within the sectors defined by its initial programme.

The content of government policy is dependent to a great extent on the upper echelons of the civil service, for it is under the direction of these people that the bills to be placed before Parliament are formulated and justified. Thus the real nucleus of power lies in the negotiations in which the wording of bills is decided upon by ministers and senior civil servants.

Parliament has in theory unlimited powers to alter the content of draft laws placed before it, but a political etiquette has emerged in the recent period of more stable governments that changes are seldom made to the main content of government bills.

The Parliament building, completed in 1931, is a national monument in the classical style that symbolizes the strength and dynamism of democracy.

Once a bill has been through its preliminary discussion it is sent to the appropriate parliamentary committee for detailed examination. This is usually an extensive process in which experts are consulted and the background to the bill and its possible

repercussions are carefully assessed. Committee proceedings take place in private and consist of discussions which tend to shape the opinions of the representatives and affect the concrete outcome in a manner which is restricted only to a minor degree by party affiliations and the pressures of publicity.

The public can follow proceedings in Parliament from the gallery of the almost circular chamber, and they are also broadcast on nationwide television.

Following this phase, the committee's report is discussed in a full parliamentary session and the final content of the law is agreed upon. If the President refuses to sign the bill into law, Parliament can approve it unchanged on a second reading, whereupon it becomes law automatically without the President's approval.

Members of Parliament have a weekly opportunity to put questions to ministers for an immediate answer, in addition to which they may present written questions, which ministers are obliged to answer within three weeks. The Speaker of Parliament and his deputies may also, at their own discretion, arrange discussions on matters of topical interest raised by members.

Parliamentary supervision of preparatory work and decisions regarding matters to be discussed in the European Union is concentrated in the Grand Committee, to which the Prime Minister reports in advance on matters to be raised in the European Council. He is then obliged to take the committee's comments into account at the meeting and report on it to the committee afterwards.

The Grand Committee is responsible for monitoring the preparation of EU legislation, and government ministers report to it every Friday on matters in their own sector coming up for formal discussion during the next week. The committee will then state the opinions of Parliament on these matters. The opinions represent political guidelines to be followed by the government. The government's failure to observe the will of Parliament may lead to a vote of no confidence and in extreme cases to the

government's resignation. This means that Parliament occupies a stronger position in the handling of EU matters than is the case in many other countries.

THE PRESIDENT

The President of Finland is the head of state, who is elected by direct popular vote for a six-year term of office, with a maximum of two terms. The President is responsible for foreign and security policy, but is bound under the constitution to collaborate with the government in these matters. Consultations between them usually lead to a consensus of opinion, but if this cannot be achieved the government's view is adopted as official policy.

The President appoints the top civil servants, officers of the Defence Forces and the judges of the Supreme Court on the basis of proposals from the government and is also Commander of the Defence Forces, although this position may be delegated to another Finnish citizen on the suggestion of the government. The President also approves all statutes related to administrative matters and the implementation of laws.

The President is not responsible to Parliament, but in fact all presidential functions require the assent of the government, which must enjoy the confidence of Parliament. The President is in principle the highest authority in the administration, but in practice every decision is made at the suggestion of a government minister and becomes law only when that minister has ratified it.

The country's political structure is dominated by an equilibrium between the three major parties and a broad-based, virtually tacit unanimity regarding the fundamental structure of the welfare state.

POLITICAL PARTIES

Following the Civil War that ensued after Finland's declaration of independence, the Social Democrats set out to guide the labour movement along a path of western democracy. They still receive economic and ideological support from a reasonably powerful trade union organization. Meanwhile, the interests of the agrarian population were promoted by a separate party which eventually developed into the Centre Party and has as such retained its political influence in spite of the decline in the size of the agrarian population some time ago to the low level found in most other European countries. The third major political grouping is the conservative National Coalition Party, which has developed from an organ of the middle-class urban population into a supporter of the interests of white-collar employees.

Alongside these three major parties there are three medium-sized parties in Parliament, namely the Left-Wing Alliance, the

The Finns are excellent at organizing themselves into all manner of societies and associations to pursue particular hobbies or causes. They are accustomed to teamwork and readily sign on for mass sports and fitness events, typically in groups representing workplaces or circles of friends. One of the more popular of the light-hearted events is the 'Women's Ten', an annual 10-kilometre run in Helsinki in which thousands of women take part.

political successor of the once mighty Communist Party, the Greens, who have gained in strength consistently since the early 1980s, and the Swedish People's Party, which upholds the interests of the country's linguistic minority. There are also usually two to four small parties represented in Parliament, either the "Last of the Mohicans", in other words a party or parties in decline, or pioneers of new ideas attempting to gain a footing. The system of proportional representation makes it very difficult for these small groups to develop the critical mass necessary for catching up with the medium-sized parties.

THREE-WAY BARGAINING

In the 1960s, the central organizations of trade unions and employers began to hold negotiations to produce umbrella agreements on pay and working conditions that would create the basic outlines for contracts in all sectors of the economy. Gradually these consultations have been extended to cover matters of taxation and social policy. The structural changes that have taken place in the economy and the globalization of the markets have nevertheless detracted greatly from the chances of achieving centralized pay agreements in recent years.

A permanent negotiating machinery has nevertheless been established in which the government has come to play an increasingly prominent role. The decisions reached by the process of three-way bargaining are in formal terms no more than

The maternity package is a free of charge gift provided for the parents of every newborn child. It contains lots of items selected to help parents to cope with a new addition to the family.

agreements between organizations, but in practice they are taken as binding.

This means, in fact, that the organizations concerned have taken it upon themselves to exercise powers that originally belonged to Parliament, even though the legislation required by their mutual agreements is naturally dependent in a formal sense on parliamentary procedures.

The strong negotiating position of the trade unions is partly a product of the traditionally high union membership, which

is diminishing slightly, although even today the unions account for just over 71% of the labour force. The pressure to join a union is great, as the entitlement to earnings-related unemployment benefits is dependent on contributions to an unemployment fund and all the largest such funds are run by the unions. An independent unemployment fund that is not attached to any union has now grown up alongside these, however. Union dues are deducted directly from employees' wages and paid over to the unions by the employers. All agreements concluded between trade unions and employers apply equally well to non-union workers.

There is also a network of other professional organizations in Finland alongside the trade unions that are similarly devoted to protecting the rights and interests of their members. These organizations are not entitled to enter into formal agreements or contracts, but the most powerful ones in the field of research and economic policy are able to influence developments in the long term through public opinion and lobbying.

The local authorities are responsible for public welfare in their own districts, arranging matters such as statutory educational, medical and child care services. New joint activities for mothers with young children are becoming available through special amenities including mother-and-baby cafes, cinemas and museums.

Finland is divided administratively into five provinces and 416 local government districts, or municipalities. The latter are declining rapidly in number at present as a consequence of mergers undertaken for economic reasons. The state has passed responsibility for the

LOCAL GOVERNMENT

ÅLAND

The province of Åland, also known as the Åland Islands, has a special status in Finland as a demilitarized, self-governing region. The basis for this rests in the Treaty of Paris that ended the Crimean War in 1856. Their demilitarized, neutral status was confirmed and extended in subsequent treaties, in particular the multilateral Åland Convention concluded in 1921 on the initiative of the League of Nations.

The autonomous status of Åland is also based on a decision of the Council of the League of Nations in 1921 that resolved a dispute between Finland and Sweden over the islands and is intended to guarantee the preservation of the local language, which is Swedish, and the local culture. Åland has its own representative on the Nordic Council, as have the other Nordic self-governing areas, the Faroe Islands and Greenland.

The province of Åland consists of more than 6 500 islands and skerries, of which 6 400 are larger than 3 000 m². The current population of 65 000 live on only 65 islands, and over 40% live in the only town, the capital, Mariehamn.

Nature is perhaps Åland's greatest attraction. The climate is milder than elsewhere in Finland, the bird population is exceptionally varied and the flora very distinctive.

The special character of the islands has inspired painters, writers and musicians over the centuries, and today they attract many people interested in sailing, traditional boat-building, fishing, cycling, summer cultural events and historical ruins.

The Åland Islands form an autonomous province of Finland with its own flag and postage stamps, and Swedish as its only official language. The beauty of the islands and their many interesting historical sites attract large numbers of visitors from the mainland and from abroad.

provision of most welfare services on to the local authorities and pays them contributions towards the production of these services in relation to their ability to bear the costs. Thus government subsidies make up about 36% of the incomes of most local authorities.

The main source of local government funding is local taxation, levied at a flat rate as a percentage of income in connection with state taxation, the rate for which is progressive. Each local authority sets its own rate of tax on the basis of its estimated expenditure.

The local authorities decide independently on the use made of their incomes for the production of services, the main categories of which are health services and hospitals, compulsory education, social services and fire and rescue services. They also maintain library services, which are among the most comprehensive and efficient in the world, and they exercise considerable power s over areal planning.

Some aspects of infrastructure maintenance, e.g. water supplies, sewerage, port and harbour services, and to some extent district heating and electricity supplies, are organized in the form of local authority business enterprises which obtain their income directly from consumers. The power of decision in matters of taxation, finance, administration and planning lies with the local council, which is elected every four years on the principle of universal suffrage. Foreigners are also allowed to vote in local government elections in the municipalities where they live.

Local politics are dominated by branches of the larger national political parties, but many councils have significant groups of independents or representatives of local interests. A large number of members of parliament are also customarily elected to local councils, where they often occupy high positions.

The Finnish judicial system is a classic example of the doctrine of the distribution of power in matters of legislation and administration, its only point of contact with the administrative system being the

JUSTICE

fact that the highest judges are appointed by the President, after which it is in practice impossible to dismiss them.

The general system of courts operates at three levels, of which the highest level deals only with cases that may set a precedent or in which an obvious technical error has occurred in an earlier hearing. The Office of the Prosecutor General operates independently of both the courts and the police. In addition to the general pattern of courts there are various specialized courts that rule on matters such as housing, insurance, water rights and marketing, and a series of administrative courts that deal with complaints regarding administrative procedures.

Cases brought against government ministers or higher officials in the judiciary are heard in a separate High Court of Impeachment appointed by Parliament. The decision to pursue

legal action against a minister in this way is taken by Parliament, but the threshold for doing so is so high that the system cannot be manipulated for purely political ends. Cases of impeachment are extremely rare.

The highest guardian of legality in the country is the Chancellor of Justice, who is present at all cabinet meetings and can intervene at any moment if the form or content of any proposed resolution is at variance with existing legislation. Citizens who have experienced injustice at the hands of the authorities can appeal directly to the Chancellor.

Parliament has its own ombudsman who supervises the legality of the legislative authorities and can similarly deal with complaints from the public. The ombudsman is also responsible for justice in the country's prisons and in the Defence Forces.

Open-air markets, both permanent and seasonal, are an essential part of Finnish life. Grandmothers looking after babies, members of parliament, and local celebrities sit side by side in the cafes, drinking coffee and eating doughnuts. A good conversation will soon put the world to rights, as here in Turku Market Place.

DEFENCE National defence is organized in a regional system covering the whole territory of Finland and operating on the basis of general military service. A very high proportion of each age-group of men enter military service, 82%, which means an annual intake of about 30 000. Military service is voluntary for women, and about 500 a year take up this option and receive the same training as the male conscripts. The period of service is one year for those wishing to qualify as officers in the reserves and somewhat less for NCOs and the lower ranks.

The purpose of the military training is to provide troops to be mobilized in the event of war, at which time every person registered in the reserves would have a designated role. Refresher courses are held regularly for reservists, who constitute a trained force of about half a million, or almost 10% of the total population, the highest proportion of any country in Europe.

In wartime the majority of reservists would be deployed in the regional defence system, in which active units should be capable of operating independently. In addition, three rapid deployment brigades can be formed for deployment to defend major industrial and administrative centres against strategic strikes. The mobilization strength of the Defence Forces will decrease to just over 350 000 during the present decade and the declining trend will continue after 2010.

The Air Force operates mainly with American F-18 fighters and the main armoured vehicles used by the ground forces are reconditioned German Leopard tanks. The core of the coastal defence system is formed by Swedish-made marine target missiles fired from fast naval vessels or from land-based mobile launching pads, an advanced underwater sonar system and an effective network of sea mines. Finland has one of the best-armed artillery divisions in Europe.

This conscription-based defence system relies to a significant extent on support from public opinion. Opinion polls reveal that about 77% of respondents would be willing to take up arms to

The island fortress of Suomenlinna was built by the Swedes in the eighteenth century to defend their easternmost province, Finland. Although it failed in this task, it remained an important military installation for a long time and still has a limited military role. Now one of the most popular tourist sites in the country, with restaurants and museums, it is included on the UNESCO World Heritage List.

defend their country in all situations. Finland's security policy is based on military non-alliance, but the possibility of applying for NATO membership has not been excluded.

The fact that public opinion is fairly firmly against military alignment indicates that, for the first time in centuries, the Finns have a true measure of security in their lives in a military sense, but paradoxically, it also suggests that popular opinion has not yet comprehended how deeply Finland is now committed to UN, EU and NATO military peacekeeping and crisis management operations.

The largest Finnish peacekeeping contingent is that assigned to the K-For troops in Kosovo, brigade-level units in which have twice been commanded by a Finnish general. Finns are also engaged in military observer or police duties in Afghanistan, Bosnia, the Lebanon, Eritrea, Ethiopia and Kashmir.

Jukka Tarkka, D.Soc.Sc., is a historian, columnist and political commentator.

Young Finnish men – and some young women, too, nowadays – spend up to about a year in national service. For males who are conscientious objectors, the alternative is community service.

6

Nature and Population

Extreme experiences, diversity and security. A land of mighty fells and low-lying meadows, forests and peatlands, lake regions and islands. A landscape that changes with the four seasons. The annual range of temperature can be more than 80 degrees celsius. A modern, smoothly functioning, technological society in spite of harsh climatic conditions.

The 50 days or so in winter when the sun never rises and the couple of months of light summer nights when it does not set are two extreme phenomena experienced in the north of Lapland. In southern Finland the days are reasonably light even in winter, and the permanent snow cover that usually forms by December increases the brightness by day.

EXTREME EXPERIENCES AND VARIED IMPRESSIONS

Finland is in many ways a land of extremes. Temperatures can fluctuate over a range of more than 80°C in the course of a year, and the sun can remain below the horizon for more than 50 days around midwinter in the north, only to shine day and night for more than two months in summer. It is a land of mighty fells, forests and bogs stretching as far as the eye can see, labyrinthine lake areas and lush, leafy woodlands – and all these landscapes alter in appearance with the time of day and season of the year.

The Finns are largely western Europeans in their roots, culture and religion, although with strong eastern influences. There are many places in the north where the population is as sparsely distributed as in Siberia, and reindeer herding is still a viable occupation, whereas the people of the Helsinki conurbation live busy, urbane lives just like those in the world's other metropolises. In spite of all these variations, however, Finland as an entity is an advanced information society with high standards of democracy, technology and welfare services.

All this means that the country can offer its visitors the sense of being in a modern-day periphery, a feeling of peace and the thrill of nature under conditions in which the basic necessities of life are catered for, everything works and security is assured.

In spite of its small population, Finland is a medium-sized European country in terms of area. Almost a fourth of that area lies north of the Arctic Circle, so that it competes with Iceland as the most northerly independent country in the world, but at the same time it borders on the Baltic Sea in the south and west, giving it direct access to continental Europe by ship. The fractured coastline in the south-west gradually gives way to a vast archipelago which is exceptional on account of the sheer number of islands, their varying sizes and their diversity.

Although it has no real mountain ranges, Finland has a landscape that typically shows a great deal of small-scale variation in relief. Most of the country is a plain that slopes away gently towards the south and south-east, while the landscapes in the east are dominated by hills and lakes and the undulating country of the central region gives way westwards to the flat coastal plains of Ostrobothnia and elsewhere on the coast to hilly or upland terrain. In Lapland the stark barrenness of the fells is interrupted by deep canyons and raging rivers. The most mountainous area of all is the "arm" of Enontekiö, which stretches into the Scandes range and features the country's highest point, Halti (1328 m).

Most of the bedrock of Finland was laid down some 2.8–1.8

A COUNTRY OF MANY FACETS

The broad hills of Lapland are called fells rather than mountains. The fells form wild, majestic landscapes in the far north. The fells of Malla are located at Kilpisjärvi at the outermost point of the northwestern "arm" of Finland, close to the borders with Sweden and Norway.

billion years ago, but the overlying deposits are relatively recent, as 20000 years ago the whole area was still covered by the glacier of the last Ice Age, which reached a thickness of three kilometres in places. The ice had retreated entirely by around 9000 years ago, allowing living things to re-establish themselves, and it is interesting that man probably came to this area earlier than did either of the main forest trees, pine or spruce. We are still reminded of the Ice Age by the phenomenon of land uplift, which is continually shaping the landscape and adds about 700 ha to the country's land area every year.

Finland has the greatest proportion of lakes of any country in the world, as there are almost 188 000 altogether and they account for about a tenth of the total surface area, reaching one fourth and even over a half in some places in the east. The rivers, on the other hand, are usually short and carry relatively small volumes of water, as the watersheds are not located very far away from the coast. The main watershed is the area known as Maanselkä, which separates the river and lake systems flowing into the Baltic Sea (91% of total discharge) from those flowing into the Arctic Ocean and the White Sea (9%).

The natural environment of the lake areas is something quite remarkable. The ancient bedrock, the effects of the Ice Age and the later influence of land uplift have combined to create a labyrinthine system of waterways with constantly varying scenery in which

the lakes are joined together by innumerable narrow straits and stretches of river. There are also almost 100 000 forested islands, often with steep, rocky shores, giving a total length of shoreline of practically 200 000 km.

Finland lies on the western edge of the coniferous forest zone, or taiga, that covers the whole northern part of Eurasia, and although the country stretches from the northern boundary of the oak zone to the bare subarctic fell tops, the forests typically contain only a small number of tree species, of which only pine, spruce and birch, and to some extent alder and aspen, are of any commercial importance. Over two thirds of the land area is covered by productive forest, giving Finland the highest density of forests in Europe, while no other country in the world can match it for the proportion of bogs. The majority of the country's animals are species typical of the boreal coniferous zone, such as the elk and the national animal, the bear. The region also has representatives of the Arctic faunal type in the north and the European faunal type in the south. On account of the recent origins of the fauna, there are only a few endemic species, such as the Saimaa Ringed Seal, the world's rarest seal species, which is a relic from the period immediately following the Ice Age and nowadays warrants a conservation programme of its own.

The national animal, the bear, is a shy inhabitant of the more remote forests, but berry pickers may occasionally catch a glimpse of one at the best picking sites in late summer.

The Finnish climate is much milder than one would expect from the country's northerly location, as it is affected by the presence of the Baltic Sea and vast lake areas and by the westerly winds, which bring air warmed by the Gulf Stream from the Atlantic. The result is that mean temperatures are 6–10 degrees higher on average than at comparable latitudes elsewhere.

WESTERLY WINDS, WINTER DARKNESS AND LIGHT SUMMER NIGHTS

Finland belongs to a sector of the region with a snowy forest climate that has cold, damp winters, although continental air masses from the east can enter the area from time to time, causing cold, frosty spells in winter and heat waves in summer. The northern parts of the country can have temperatures as low as -50°C in cold winters, whilst figures of over +30°C may be recorded in many places during the short summers. In the far north of Lapland the sun remains below the horizon for 52 days in midwinter, whereas in the south the shortest day still lasts six hours. The light summers more than make up for the dark winters, however, for there are 19 hours of daylight on the south coast at Midsummer and the sun is visible uninterruptedly for 67 days at Nuorgam in the extreme north. It is often difficult for foreigners to understand the great variations in climate and light conditions in Finland.

Precipitation is received at all seasons in the year, but is not divided equally among them. It is often said that the coastal strip of south-western Finland and Ostrobothnia does not have enough rain in the early summer to satisfy the farmers, whereas there is often too much rain towards the end of the summer. The growing season, defined as the period during which temperatures are constantly above 5°C, is about two months longer in the south than in the north, but the effect is evened out somewhat by the light nights in the north. It is the more or less constant daylight that makes the wild berries that grow in Finland so delicious.

NATIONAL PLANTS AND ANIMALS

National flower: lily of the valley
National animal: bear
National tree: birch
National bird: swan
National fish: perch
National insect: ladybird

The character of the Finnish people has been shaped to a great extent by the harsh climate, the sparse settlement and the country's remote location. Their way of life has traditionally involved a struggle to achieve self-sufficiency, disciplined action and a capacity for hard work, since up to the end of the nineteenth century most people lived close to the poverty line and many had to eke out their bread flour by adding ground pine bark to it even in good years. When life was a constant matter of preparing for the worst, the largely agrarian society did not take kindly to those of a playful or innovative disposition, but favoured dogged labourers. The Finns have traditionally had a strong belief in education, the authorities and the judicial system.

Finland has a wealth of natural resources that it can exploit as raw materials or for energy generation. Most important of all are its forests, which formed the basis of the first wave of industrialization in the late nineteenth century. Its total timber reserves of more than 2000 million m³ are the greatest in Europe after those of Russia, Sweden and Germany, and the annual growth of the forests amounts to almost 80 million m³. Another renewable natural resource is water, which is used as a source of hydroelectric power as well as for household supplies and in industrial processes.

NATURAL RESOURCES AND NATURE CONSERVATION

The bedrock contains a number of rock types that are suitable as industrial raw materials, and also a wide range of ores. Deposits of gold and diamonds have been discovered in recent times. The most valuable materials that can be extracted from the loose deposits are gravel, sand, clay and peat, to the extent that Finland has the third largest peat reserves in the world after Russia and Canada.

Although the environment is relatively unpolluted and in a natural state by international standards, increasing attention is being paid to conservation, one major aspect of which is protection of the country's lakes, rivers and sea areas, as the majority of the

RIGHTS OF ACCESS IN NATURE

All citizens are entitled to enjoy nature within certain limits without permission from landowners. The rights of access allow one:

· to move about in the countryside on foot, on skis or by bicycle other than in the yard of a house or in fields, meadows or planted areas where this could cause damage,

· to stay temporarily, e.g. overnight in a tent, at a place where such movement is permitted, provided that the place is sufficiently far away from any dwellings,

· to pick wild berries, mushrooms and flowers, provided these are not protected species, and

· to travel on, swim in or wash oneself in a lake, stream or river or at a sea shore and to move about on ice formed on any such body of water.

The rights of access in Åland differ somewhat from those elsewhere in Finland, and some of the above rights may be reserved exclusively for local residents.

pollutants entering the environment end up in these and they are particularly susceptible to damage because they are in general very shallow.

Conservation areas of various kinds have been set up, the most important of which are the 19 nature reserves, where access is subject to a permit, and the 35 national parks, which are intended for research, teaching and recreational purposes. There are also areas set aside for the protection of bogs, fresh herb-rich forests, shores, ancient forests and seals, and numerous nature conservation areas created by private citizens on their own land. Finland approved the EU's Natura 2000 nature conservation programme in 1998, and about 14% of the country's land area now falls within its provisions.

POPULATION   There were evidently people living in the area of present-day Finland over 120 000 years ago, although human settlement was later forced to retreat on account of the Ice Age. The earliest

ancestors of the Finns set foot on the territory that emerged from beneath the ice some time between 9000 and 8000 BC, presumably coming from at least two directions, the east and the south, and the land has been inhabited continuously ever since. New population groups have come here from various quarters, but they have all merged in with the existing inhabitants. Broadly speaking, the Finnish population has derived three fourths of its genes from Baltic-Germanic stock and one fourth from the east.

The population of Finland passed the three million mark in 1914 and reached four million in 1950. The high birth rate in the years following the Second World War meant that the population grew rapidly for some time, but a decline in the birth rate and massive emigration to Sweden in the 1960s caused the total to fall at times. A new rise took place in the 1980s, however, with the return of many of the emigrants and a fresh increase in the birth rate, since when population growth has settled at about the same level as in other European countries. The total passed five million

Nature conservation is taken very seriously. Regulations governing national parks and various other protection orders place restrictions on hunting and access to certain parts of the countryside. On the other hand, properly supervised hunting and trapping of game birds and animals is a means of keeping wildlife populations in check.

in 1991 and was approximately 5 280 000 in December 2006.

A typical feature of the Finnish population is a high proportion of people of active working age and a gradual ageing of the whole demographic structure. Children (0–14 years) make up just under a fifth of the total, persons of retirement age (over 65 years) more than 15% and those of working age slightly more than two thirds. With retirement taking place in practice at an average age of just under 60 and the population as a whole becoming older, the question has arisen as to how it will be possible to meet the necessary pension bill in the future. Thus greater flexibility has been introduced into the pensions system and people are being encouraged to remain at work longer.

The fact that women account for over 51% of the population is due chiefly to the higher mortality among men, as more boys than girls are born virtually every year. This also means that two thirds of the retired people are women. The position of women in society has improved since they have been able to concentrate on a career of their own as well as raising a family, and over a half of all university students nowadays are women.

The population includes almost 2.5 million unmarried persons and just under 2 million who are married. Over 80% of families with children have just one or two children, but couples

The population is ageing. Early retirement is widespread as people hope to enjoy their retirement to the full. Pensioners are entitled to discounts on admission to places such as swimming pools, theatres and museums.

without children have become more common, now accounting for almost a half of all families. Living alone is more common in towns than in the countryside. A new law passed in 2002 allows couples of the same sex to register their relationship and, with certain exceptions, guarantees them the same rights and obligations as married couples.

Great changes in family structure have taken place in recent decades. Almost a half of all marriages nowadays end in divorce, common law marriages have gained acceptance and there are increasing numbers of families resulting from remarriages, which may include children of one or both of the spouses from a previous marriage as well as those from their current marriage. Even so, it is fair to say that the Finns place great value on dependability, faithfulness and honesty in a relationship.

The national bird is the swan which has been immortalized in the poems of Runeberg, in numerous musical compositions and most recently on the Finnish euro coins.

In the majority of Finnish families both parents go out to work. This means that fathers take a more active part in looking after the children than they used to and make decisions regarding the children and the life of the family together with their wives or partners. It is most important that both parents should take part in bringing up the children, and weekends are usually spent together in this way. Other institutions involved in children's education are the day nurseries and schools, and constant discussions take place over the division of responsibilities between these and the home.

The Finnish population is relatively homogeneous, with the Sámi and Romany groups as the only original ethnic minorities. The majority of the approximately 6500 Sámi live in their traditional home areas in the northern parts of Lapland, while the population of some 10 000 Romany is distributed more evenly over the whole country. The proportion of people born outside the country is one of the lowest in Europe, as they amounted to just under 122 000 in 2006. The number of people from the area of the former Soviet Union has increased most markedly in recent times, while refugees have been accepted to a limited extent, partly through agreed quotas and partly through the granting of asylum to individual applicants. The largest groups of refugees are those from Somalia, the former Yugoslavia, Iran and Iraq.

The official languages are Finnish and Swedish, and also Sámi in this group's home area. Finnish, which belongs to the Finno-Ugric branch of the Uralic languages and is spoken by almost 92% of the population, is full of fine nuances, shades of meaning that are difficult to define and expressions that are close to nature, and it is perhaps precisely because of this special character of the language that the most famous Finnish novel, Aleksis Kivi's Seven Brothers, has never really been successful in translation. Finnish is spoken very little outside Finland, but it can be studied nowadays in numerous universities throughout the world.

More than 5% of the population, mainly living on the south and west coasts and in the Åland Islands, speak Swedish as their native language, but government services are available in both languages throughout the country and Swedish speakers are able to study right up to university level in their own language. There is a constant polemic going on concerning the role of Swedish, in spite of its strong juridical status: some people believe its position should be strengthened and others would like to do away with "compulsory Swedish".

The rapid increase in international relations and an influx of immigrants has made Finnish society far more diverse linguistically than it used to be. English is by far the most widely understood among the foreign languages, but skills in other languages have improved, too. Dozens of languages are taught as the native tongues of children in schools, especially in the Helsinki region, where many families are bilingual or multilingual.

A LAND OF LUTHERANS

The Evangelical Lutheran Church of Finland and the Orthodox Church of Finland are established churches with a legal status that allows them certain rights, including the levying of church taxes. Together with the other Nordic countries, Finland forms one of the most pronouncedly Lutheran areas of the world. Over 82% of the population belong to this church, which is headed by the Archbishop of Turku and is divided into nine dioceses, of which that of Porvoo (Borgå) is responsible for all the Swedish-speaking parishes in the country. Research has shown that members go to church twice a year on average, active membership being most common in the older age groups. The first women priests were ordained in 1988.

The "Church in the Rock" is one of the favourite attractions for visitors to Helsinki and is extremely popular for concerts because of its fine acoustics and impressive interior.

The Orthodox Church of Finland, which belongs to the Patriarchate of Constantinople, is divided into three dioceses, Helsinki, Karelia and Oulu, and is led by the Archbishop, whose residence is in Kuopio. Although only about 1.1% of the population belong to this church, it contributes greatly to the country's spiritual and intellectual life. Its ancient ascetic tradition is kept up in the Convent of Lintula and the Monastery of New Valamo, and the latter also caters extensively for pilgrims and other visitors.

Over 9000 people in Finland belong to the Roman Catholic Church, about 1600 to the Jewish congregations and a small number among the Muslim population, about 2300, are affiliated to official Islamic communities.

Although there has been freedom of religious observance since 1923, the number of declared atheists is low, as even among the 15% of the population who do not belong to the established churches about a half would regard themselves as Christians.

AN UNEVEN PATTERN OF SETTLEMENT

Finland is the third most sparsely populated country in Europe after Iceland and Norway, with a mean population density of 17.4 inhabitants per km of land area in December 2006. Although it is settled to some extent throughout, there are great variations in the density of this settlement. The province of Lapland, for instance, which covers the northernmost part of the country, has only two inhabitants per square kilometre, whereas the Helsinki conurbation on the south coast is rapidly growing into a continuous metropolitan area with almost 1 500 000 inhabitants.

The next largest cities after Helsinki (population 565 000) are Espoo (235 000), Tampere, the largest inland city in the Nordic region (over 205 000), Vantaa (almost 190 000) and Turku, which was the seat of administration until 1812 (over 175 000). Altogether Finland had 416 municipalities in January 2007, of which 64 were classified as urban, a further 74 as densely inhabited and 278 as rural.

Alongside this system, the country is divided for general administrative purposes into five provinces, together with the

The Northern Lights

The Northern Lights, or *Aurora Borealis*, are light effects visible in the night sky of areas close to the magnetic pole. They are caused by charged particles carried by solar winds colliding at high speed with atoms and molecules in the Earth's atmosphere. As a result, the atoms and molecules gain a charge and subsequently emit a light quantum on releasing it.

The most common colour for the Northern Lights is a yellowish green, which is derived from oxygen atoms and is usually released at altitudes of 90–150 km. The red light often seen above this is also from oxygen atoms, while blue or violet light is from nitrogen ions. The Northern Lights can occur equally well in summer as in winter, but cannot be seen in summer because the sky is usually too light. Finland is one of the leading countries for research into the Northern Lights. They can be seen at their best late in the evening in the northern parts of Lapland, although they are also clearly visible in the south of the country.

Among the many varieties of water sport, canoeing has gained in popularity from year to year alongside the more traditional sport of sailing. The canoeist has a full range of activities to choose from, from the quiet observation of nature to extreme tests of white-water skills and strength on stretches of natural rapids.

autonomous province of Åland, each with its own administration headed by a governor, and further into assize court districts and local government municipalities. There is also a system of 20 economically, functionally and culturally distinct regions, partly based on the historical division of Finland was divided into the provinces of Varsinais-Suomi (Finland Proper), Åland, Uusimaa, Häme, Satakunta, Savo, Karelia, Ostrobothnia and Lapland.

Living conditions are a matter of far more concern for people living in a northerly country such as this than they are in places with a milder climate. The houses, which have on average been built more recently than those in any other country in Europe, have to be well insulated, efficiently heated and provided with double or triple glazing to conserve energy and reduce heating costs. Well over half of the total of nearly 2.7 million dwellings are occupier-owned, and although the number of rented dwellings has increased, there remain fewer of them, and of dwellings provided by an employer or linked to an official position, than in most other western European countries.

The majority of Finns would like to live in a private house standing in its own garden, and there has been a considerable increase in the proportion of such houses being built in recent times. Many families with children prefer to move out of urban centres into the suburbs in order to live more spaciously. New house building has still not been able to keep up with demand, however, as almost a million people may be said to be living in cramped conditions by the generally accepted European standard of more than one room per inhabitant, excluding the kitchen.

The Finns are very fond of nature and like to be in peace. After the rigours of the cold, dark winter, they are happy to spend the warm, light summer months out of doors, often at their holiday cabins, of which there are over 470 000, mostly near the sea shore or close to lakes. With increasing leisure time, more and more cabins are being fitted out for year-round use, and it is not uncommon for retired people to sell their home in town and move entirely to their second home in the country, often close to their childhood surroundings.

Another factor that raises living standards is the possession of a sauna, of which there are over two million altogether. This is a sacred matter for the Finns, rather like the tea ceremony for the Japanese. The sauna has a cleansing and relaxing effect, especially if it is possible to plunge into cool water afterwards. The wildest sauna enthusiasts may roll in the snow in winter or swim in a hole in the ice. The first world championships for swimming in a pool cut in ice were held in Helsinki in February 2000.

Being a northerly country, Finland does not suffer from the problems of mass tourism. Its attractions lie in its stable, safe social conditions, its excellent infrastructure, the good command

TRAVEL

of languages shown by its tourism personnel, its sparse settlement and a diverse natural environment that is free of pollution and offers wonderful opportunities for visitors interested in nature, cultural events and extreme experiences. Especially notable are the many summer musical gatherings, such as the Savonlinna Opera Festival, the Kuhmo Chamber Music Festival and Pori Jazz, which feature top class international artists performing in authentic Finnish surroundings.

The forests, lakes and rivers provide excellent conditions for outdoor adventures, allowing hikers, canoeists and fishermen infinite opportunities to pit their strength against the forces of nature. The Kainuu region in particular is renowned for its safaris to watch bears and other animals in the wild. You can also enjoy the natural scenery of the lake areas by taking an excursion on one of the traditional steamships, rent one of the thousands of holiday cottages, or experience the magic of playing golf by the light of the midnight sun.

Finland has also been growing in popularity as a winter holiday destination, the main activities being cross-country and downhill skiing, snowboarding and snowmobile or dog team safaris. Many of the winter sports centres also have high quality spas, as spa hotels are another field in which Finland is the leading operator in the Nordic region. The main attraction towards the end of the year is the world's only genuine Santa Claus, who welcomes tens of thousands of visitors, large and small, from Britain alone every year.

One of the oldest tourist sights in the country is the hill of Aavasaksa, a granite outcrop which rises up sharply from the Tornio River valley on the western border of Lapland, offering magnificent views, especially of the midnight sun at Midsummer. Another place worth visiting is the Verla Factory Museum in the south-east, a fine example of Finland's early industrial history in the form of a well preserved pulp and board mill from the late nineteenth century which was placed on the UNESCO World Heritage List in 1996.

By far the most popular venue for tourists, however, is Helsinki, which has more visitors each year than the whole of Lapland. Its architecture reflects the history of this country and its position between east and west, and its streets buzz with the international, multicultural flavour that began to emerge here towards the end of the twentieth century. It has a lively programme of cultural events of all kinds, although the most popular places are evidently the Linnanmäki funfair, with more than 1.3 million visitors a year, and the island fortress of Suomenlinna just off the coast.

As we all know, Santa Claus lives at Korvatunturi in Finnish Lapland, from where he sets out every Christmas to deliver presents to all the well-behaved children and grown-ups in the world.

Finland is a popular country for holding conferences, not least because the many meetings of world leaders held here have demonstrated that the Finns are experts at providing good facilities and ensuring the safety of delegates. The good "gateway" transport connections also mean that it is easy to combine conferences with holiday excursions to the other Nordic countries, the Baltic States and Russia, especially St. Petersburg. Connections with Asia are also excellent, as the shortest air route between any EU capital and Asia is that from Helsinki.

Allan Tiitta, Ph.D., has spent his whole career in the field of academic research and publishing. He has written numerous works on Finland, its people, and their history.

7

Finland within

Finland has always adapted well to social and historical upheavals. It is a country small in population with a firm belief in consensus and concerted action. There was rapid transformation from a remote agricultural country to an affluent, urbanized society. Good relations with its neighbours helped Finland to survive in the shadow of the delicate balance of power in Europe. It is a land of vast contrasts with a calmness that can be sensed.

Finnish technology has faced up successfully to one of its greatest challenges, that of keeping coastal waters open to shipping all year round.

SUOMI-MYTHS AND REALITY

Every nation can claim its own big story, the metanarrative that somehow orders and explains collective knowledge and experience. The Finnish master narrative is associated with nationhood and with gaining independence. Finland's nationhood has an interesting Janus character to it. The two faces have had to look in opposite directions and to draw stimuli and inspiration from many points of the compass. For six centuries, Finland was annexed to Sweden – the Österlanden or "eastern lands" of the rulers in Stockholm. The country has been under the influence of western European culture at least since the 12th century. The years from 1809 to 1917, as part of the Russian Empire, in turn engendered a strong and distinctive relationship with the huge eastern state and its culture. Finland thereafter took its place as an independent nation in the marchlands between Sweden and Russia. The country has been both a bastion of the west and part of the sphere of interest of the east. Geography, a latitude well above 60°N, and the severity of the climate have all been turned to good use at some point. Finland is the only country in central or eastern Europe that was able to follow its chosen political path during the 20th century without interruption or occupation.

Finns have grown accustomed to philosophising on their "national identity", and to adapting their image of themselves to suit changing external pressures. It has been customary to speak of the country through a whole string of mythical expressions. Back in the early 19th century there was the mythical image of a frontier land providing a bridge between East and West, as a western shield of Christianity, even as a northerly Athens of civilisation and culture. In the following century the *Land of a Thousand Lakes* was served up to represent the extraction and refining of the *green gold* of our forests – the core expertise of the pulp and paper industry. Finns have been seen as a taciturn people, quite capable – in Bertolt Brecht's famous remark – of *remaining silent in two languages*, Finnish and Swedish. Finnish traits such as *frugality*, *severity*, *tenacity*, and the virtue of *sisu* or "true grit" are still very much alive and kicking. Mythical properties have been sought from the natural surroundings, from the harsh winter, the explosive changing of the seasons, the Northern Lights; and from a presumed heroic prehistory made manifest in the epic poem *Kalevala*. Fantasy and fairytale, too, have taken on a mythical dimension when Finland is spoken of today as *The Land of Santa Claus*. The northern location

"He doesn't talk and doesn't kiss" – this stereotype of the strong, silent Finnish male is still in use today. The first realistic portrayal of the Finnish man was the raw masculinity of the heroes of Aleksis Kivi's novel *The Seven Brothers* (1870), the first work of fiction published in Finnish. The successful presence in international ice hockey upholds the image in a modern form.

and its strongly peripheral quality were associated with Finland and Finnishness particularly during the Cold War years. It was an image based on the country's setting in a neutral and northerly zone between opposing power blocs.

Myths are manifestations of an imagined reality. They express fragments of the collective experience. The reality is nevertheless a more nuanced matter. The relationships Finns have towards the international, national, and local space have changed as the 20th century has given way to the 21st. In the past two decades, Finland has taken its place in European communality, and has even led it on two occasions (in 1999 and 2006). Among Finns, talk of European integration was initially the liturgy of politics, the economy, and security questions. Now the cultural dimension is more to the fore, and with it cooperation among citizens. Globalisation, too, impinges on the modern Finnish everyday in many and varied ways. A whole host of conflicting narratives now cross one with another; there is no longer one mythical metatruth that can be told about Finland.

In the 20th century Finland presented itself as a social stage on which rapid movements were played out. Concepts such as transition, change, and modernisation were the order of the day. The country has morphed in the course of a hundred years from an obscure agrarian land perched at the top of Europe into one of the richest nations in the world. Historical memories are woven around this dynamic process of change and mobilisation. But there are also strong cultural continua in the image that emerges. Finnishness has ever been greatly shaped in the middle ground between nature and civilisation, between the agrarian and the urban worlds. Out of this soil, Finland has grown into a country with an enviable global reputation for basic schooling, cultural smarts, and advanced technology. It is no longer enough to lean on the old staples of extraordinary landscapes or charming natural romanticism as a recipe for success. The long history of civilisation in the region and a strong commitment to culture and education

The Finns used to look on "sauna, sisu and Sibelius" as a suitable set of symbols for the nation. The composer Jean Sibelius designed a sauna for his family, and it was there, apparently, that some of his greatest inspirations came to him. *Sisu* is Finnish for determination and willpower, dogged pursuit of one's aims, and it can also be obtained in lozenge form, sweetened with xylitol nowadays, of course.

provide the answer to the whys and wherefores of how Finland has coped and prospered as it has.

The myth of Finland's separate path has long roots. The history of independence stretches back less than a hundred years, but the basic goal had been unchanged since long before then, namely the building of an educated, democratic society and a sovereign independent state. There have been many "green", "quiet", or "industrial" revolutions in Finland over the nine decades since 1917. It has required an ability to pull together across political and social demarcation lines. What has emerged is a social cohesion and way of acting all its own. Wars, strikes, uprisings and attempted coups, political crises, recessions, and national emergencies have somehow welded the various actors into a consensus-driven battle for survival and into collaboration across the political barricades. There has been consensus to reduce income disparities, to dissolve regional differences, to eradicate social injustice, and to establish a broad unanimity in contemplating what Finland's international position should be.

Many of the strongest Suomi-myths are associated with Finland's political history and the world wars. They can still be seen burning bright in the collective memory and colouring discussion of what it is to be Finnish. What has made Finland interesting is the

Koskenkorva is Finland's own vodka, one of the favourite brands sold by Alko, the state liquor retail monopoly. An attempt to redesign the label caused an outbreak of popular protest. The peaceful rural scene on the label evokes the secure, bucolic atmosphere so sacred to all.

history and the connections, the context. The location in the middle of an ancient European divide between east and west continues to fascinate. Now the Baltic Sea is no longer a body of water that separates the four points of the compass, but one that binds them all together. The opening-up of recent years has increased interest in Northern Europe and in Finland. In comparisons, the country stands out as an original, even a challenging state. It is a cultural unity that has found its own personal way to go forward.

In the last few years there has been much debate about national and local history, about the war, about great and greater and greatest Finns, about culture, education, the countryside and the cities, and about the differing relationships with the past upheld by each succeeding generation. What is new is a pride in what is one's own. Greater weight is given to cultural knowhow, and local shades and colours show through. Music festivals and village fetes spring up everywhere, there are gatherings celebrating local traditions or local foods, and people give freely of their time and their talents in fostering this local milieu. For all the rapid social changes the country has witnessed, Finnishness remains firmly anchored in its mythical roots in the countryside. The even-handed development of provinces and regions is still seen as an important aspect of society.

In the past few years, Finland has risen to the top in international surveys of economic competitiveness. Two features above all mark the development of the recent past, namely urbanisation and the growth in national prosperity, both of which are still going on. The most recent key to success has been in technical innovations, whilst the latest investments are into the culture

There is nothing to beat a perch caught at the end of a jetty in the quiet of early morning, then fried in butter and eaten.

and content industries. Finnish expertise in manufacturing and production has its own long and mythical history. This history offers the tools for an understanding of the present-day IT and electronics surge. Not without reason is this country referred to as "technology-mad" or led by white-coated engineers: technical expertise has always been in demand in the battle against difficult natural conditions in a country where the climate hits hard. Finns are early adopters. Finland had its first private telephone company in the very earliest days of telephony. Since that time the telecommunications star pupil has always been receptive to new ideas and innovations. Nokia is no miracle; it is the result of a quite natural development.

Man does not live by technology alone, or from manufacturing or innovation. Even in the digital age, there is appreciation for nature, purity, and "green values". The relationship that Finns have with their forests, both mythical and real, is a strong one – emotional, sensual even. The forest has represented raw materials and employment, well-being and security, trade and prosperity. The forest has produced material benefits for farmers and landowners, for mill-magnates and for log-floaters of yore, for pulp & paper mill workers, and for hunters, too. The forest has also had its own mental significance. Finns still glide smoothly between two worlds and two contrasting identities, and they draw experiences and strengths from both. As a counterweight to work and stress, people seek relaxation from the summer cabin, the land and nature, often with water close at hand. There is an obvious positive symbiosis in this: different ways of life and different mentalities meet and interact. The authentic and the instinctive are there in the small, local details. The unbroken quiet of the lakeside landscape, the scent of woodsmoke from a sauna chimney, the rough bark of pines and firs, the dry squeak of hard snow underfoot, the golden early morning rays of spring sunshine, and the summer's first blueberry pie: these will all remain in perpetuity as both real and mythical symbols and strengths of what it means to be Finnish.

INFO-BOXES

COVER PHOTOGRAPHS

Liisa Suvikumpu

Marimekko

Artek

P.-O. Welin

European Commission

Aker Finnyards

FLAP

Liisa Suvikumpu

Otava

Lehtikuva/ Tor Wennström

Design House Stockholm

Moomin Characters

Nokia

FINLAND: FACTS	Finnish name Suomi
Type of state	Republic, parliamentary democracy with elections every four years
Head of state	President elected for a six-year term
Population	5.2 million 17 inhabitants per square kilometre
Official languages	Finnish (93%), Swedish (6%)
Area	5th largest country by area in Europe 338 145 square kilometres 10% water and 69% forest c. 190 000 lakes Europe's largest archipelago c. 100 000 islands 1,160 km length, 540 km width
Capital	Helsinki (1 million people in the metropolitan area including Espoo and Vantaa)
Other large towns	Tampere area (300 000), Turku area (300 000), Oulu area (200 000)
State religions	Lutheran (81%), Orthodox (2%), none (14%)
Independence	achieved in 1917
Member of the EU	since 1995
Currency	euro € (since 2002)
Economy	Exports by industry metal, engineering and electronics 60% forest products 30%, others 10% Exports by region 2004 Euro zone 30%, other EU countries 28%, other European countries 15%, Asia 15%, North America 7%, other regions 5% Principal trading partners (by order of volume) Germany, Sweden, Russia, Great Britain, USA, Netherlands, China, France, Italy, Denmark, Japan, Norway, Estonia
National epic	Kalevala
National nature symbols	bear, swan, perch, birch, lily-of-the-valley, granite
National topics	sauna (hot steam bath) salmiakki (sal ammoniac pastilles) sisu (mental strength) Koskenkorva (national vodka) sauvakävely (Nordic walking) Moomins (characters in children´s stories)